Another World

Home
from the
Sea

First published 2006
Copyright © 2006

British Library Cataloguing in Publication Data.
A catalogue record for this book is available
from the British Library.

ISBN 1-904685-12-9

Published by
The Stanborough Press Ltd,
Alma Park, Grantham, Lincs.

Printed in Thailand

Cover illustration copyright 2005 Gordon Bauwens
More of his maritime art can be seen at
<www.gbmarineart.com>

Design and layout: Steve Holden

Another World

Home
from the
Sea

'Here he lies where he longed to be;
Home is the sailor, home from the sea.'

from Robert Louis Stevenson's *Underwoods*

The Bob Smart story
by

R. M. A. Smart

Acknowledgements

I would like to thank my many friends who encouraged me during my ministry by simply saying that they liked my stories.

I would particularly like to thank Dr David Marshall who astonished me by telling me that he thought that the stories could be published. David remembers me when I turned up at his Humberside home way back in 1949 riding a Velocette 500 motorbike. I was filling in as novice under-pastor for Pastor Harold McCrow who was undergoing surgery at Hull infirmary at the time. I lodged with Mrs Stone in a tenement house right over the wall from Reckitt and Coleman's factory, famous for mustard and pickles and bath salts. I introduced her to the gourmet delicacy then called Nuttolene! Ever so humble, but the best digs I ever had. God bless her for taking in a refugee from Newbold College.

Contents

Foreword

Bob Smart spent part of World War Two as a radio officer on merchant vessels that braved the U-boat-infested Atlantic to bring vital supplies to Britain. Subsequently he served on a hospital ship in the Atlantic and the Mediterranean.

The Mercantile Marine sustained a higher rate of casualties than any of the other services. One in four merchant seamen perished. Bob's first vessel was torpedoed and sunk in the Caribbean Sea. The hospital ship on which he served was destroyed by a missile during the Anzio landings.

At the end of the war, 'a sailor home from the sea', Bob enrolled at Newbold College. Christian influences, present in the early life of this Kirkcaldy lad, had come to fruition in his decision to train for the ministry.

In training at Newbold and during his decades in ministry, Bob captivated everyone with his fascinating tales of the sea. I first met him following his graduation in 1949 when he came to pastor my home church in a seafaring community on the Humber. During his subsequent years as a pastor and an evangelist, and during his years in church leadership in Ireland and Scotland, Bob Smart drew on his colourful seaborne experiences. He brought many people to Christ, and a number of decisions to train for ministry are traced to his influence.

My contact with the Smart family was renewed in the late 1960s when, as History Master at Stanborough School, I taught Iris, daughter of Bob and Joy. Over the years that followed I attended many church gatherings in which, during his fine sermons, Bob continued to draw on the stories of his boyhood and seagoing career. By 1981 when Bob Smart preached at The Spa in Scarborough I was editor of this publishing company. It struck me then, as it had struck me before, that Bob was the finest story-teller I had ever heard. I approached Bob and urged him to consider committing his stories to print. He promised to 'think about it'. At subsequent meetings with Bob in Glasgow and Crieff he made it clear that he had not forgotten.

In the event, it took Bob and Joy's son Malcolm, a computer whiz, to get this gripping collection of stories into print. A businessman based in York, Malcolm has provided the finance for the whole project and arranged for Gordon Bauwens, a family friend and the best-known maritime artist in Britain whose work appears on the QE2, to provide the cover illustration.

All that remains for me to say is –

Enjoy!

David Marshall
Senior Editor
The Stanborough Press Ltd

Dedication

I would like to dedicate this small collection of wartime memoirs to my dear longsuffering family who have had to endure years of my story telling. I am sure that they can tell some of the tales much better than I can tell them myself now! In spite of it all, they have continued to encourage me almost until it was too late for me to write.

My deepest gratitude must go to my dear wife Joy, who has ever stuck by her sailor come home from the sea, all the way from Newbold College days.

Thanks, also, to my daughter Iris whom I took off to Ethiopia when she was only one year old; there to brave a strange land and later on help her dad understand what the local children were saying.

And finally to my son Malcolm, always faithful and supportive of his father. It was when I became nearly blind that he took over my pen and unravelled the scribble that I was making of the last chapter, finished it, and organised my book on his computer.

Chapter 1

The Harbour

The Psalmist locates the sea as being somewhere 'down'. Remember his words? 'They that go down to the sea in ships.' (Psalm 108:23.) And so it was in my Scottish hometown of Kirkcaldy; all the streets ran down-hill to the sea.

From my bedroom window, high above the seaside town, I could look across the rooftops to the Firth of Forth and the Island of Inchkeith. On this small island stood my friend, a tall white lighthouse. To me it looked like an angel, luminous with the dark clouds behind it or some-times dazzling white in the summer sunshine; like a kind of Gabriel, a shining pillar of white by day and a radiant light by night.

I was never alone in my attic bedroom. Through the window, every minute of the night, the turning beam of light swung in and out, illuminating the room again and again, saying a friendly 'hello'. Even on the gloomiest of nights when the November fogs swept eerily up the Firth from the cold North Sea and my friend was hidden from me, the deep gruff voice of his foghorn comforted me – a voice from that other world beyond the shores.

For an inquisitive little boy, who was forever riding his tricycle around the streets, all the streets of Kirkcaldy indeed ran downhill towards the sea, and, more particularly, downhill to the harbour. That was another world, that fascinating, intriguing world of ships.

Yes, it was sometimes a frightening world and yet an exciting place to which I was drawn over and over again. 'Thou shalt not go near the harbour', I was firmly admonished by my dear old caring Mum. If I can remember correctly, I think that the only time I ever experienced a hot spanked bottom was when I disobeyed that commandment. Of course it really was a very dangerous place for a little boy and his tricycle to go, but it was such an adventure!

I can still see the things that intrigued me. The deep, murky waters of the docks. (As I perilously peeped over the edge, they scared me stiff.) The big ships. (I thought they were big, anyway, as they towered above me on the quay.) I can still see all the long ropes and hawsers, and the cranes upping and downing. I can hear the noisy bustle going on all around, the steam and the smoke, and the shunting engines and the wagons going to and fro filled with everything, but especially lots and lots of coal. There was much to see and hear and smell. Yes, smell.

There were all kinds of ships and boats that fired my imagination. What role did they play in this other world? Some were elegant and brightly painted; some were dirty old rust buckets like the local dredger, but they, each one, had come from somewhere across the sea and were about to go somewhere else. From out of their deep mysterious holds came the strangest things: bales of esparto grass from North Africa for the paper mills, timber from the Baltic lands and Russia. There were strange bales of cork from Spain and barrels of linseed oil for the linoleum factories. The smell of linseed oil that came from those factories and pervaded the atmosphere of the whole town gave rise to the words of a well-known poem about Kirkcaldy. It described the approach to the town by train and gave the following directive to those who wanted to know when they neared Kirkcaldy, 'You'll know right well by the queer-like smell, the next stop's Kirkcaldy.'

The ships themselves, to that wide-eyed little boy, were personalities. Each had a name. There was that sprightly tramp with her tall black funnel with a white 'V' on it. I felt that it was not very appropriate to call her a tramp; she was beautiful. Her name was *Yendis* and she came from Hull; it said so in white letters on her counter stern. There was the *Fair Maid*, a gay, flag-festooned paddle-steamer that took holiday-makers on excursions over the Firth of Forth to Leith and Granton, the ports of Edinburgh.

From my window I could see, high on the horizon, Edinburgh Castle, on its rock above the city, over the other side of the Forth.

But it was down that Firth of Forth that I often gazed, looking out to the North Sea. What lay beyond the Bass Rock on the horizon? On very clear days I had seen ships disappear over that far horizon; first the hulls would disappear and then the funnels, sinking below the sea it seemed. My papa was away out there in Africa, an engineer building rice mills in a place with the strangest name, Sokoto. It was easy to answer my irate mum when I was questioned, 'Why did you go down again to that harbour?' 'But, Mum,' I would say, 'I was only looking for Papa's ship coming home!'

Just what did the other world have in store for me? Well, I was to begin to know that when I was all of seventeen years old.

The Psalmist knew. I could have found out from him by reading his Psalm 107, verses 23 and 24.

> 'They that go down to the sea in ships,
>   that do business in great waters;
>   these see the works of the Lord,
>   and his wonders in the deep.'

Chapter 2

Welcome to the other world

One day the sun was shining. The days of our youth always seemed to be full of sunshiny days. The summers were long and it never rained. The old town was as it always was, and the following day nothing had changed. But change it did. Suddenly we were at war with Germany.

For me there were frantic months of study at Edinburgh Wireless College, and then, on another sunny day, I stood on the quayside at Greenock, a Clyde port on the other side of Scotland. I had on a brand-new uniform and in my pocket an official note from Marconi International Communications Company, assigning me as third radio officer aboard the MV *Empire Flint*. The ship was a petrol tanker of some eight thousand tons belonging to Shell Oil, the first tanker I had ever seen. Nothing like that ever came near Kirkcaldy.

She was, at that stage, a 'light ship', no cargo aboard, and stood high in the water. I climbed aboard up the shaky iron gangway. It felt like climbing an iron cliffside. I clattered across the steel deck towards the accommodation, but before I could reach it, and before I could catch my breath from my perilous climb, I was met by the Chief Officer. He inspected my papers and immediately ordered me ashore again. My papers were incomplete; they had not yet been stamped by the Port Authorities. I was to learn that wherever there is a paper somebody has to stamp it!

The papers duly stamped and authorised, I arrived back at the quayside. Perhaps it had been about an hour of department searching and queuing since I left. To my consternation there was no *Empire Flint*. She had gone!

'Hey you!' a voice hailed me from farther down the quay. 'Are you the Sparks that was joining the *Empire Flint*? Your ship is underway. There's a boat here about to go out and collect the pilot from her. Jump aboard and we'll get you out.'

In those days the ships were suddenly called out at a moment's notice; no Blue Peter flags to say that we sailed in twenty-four hours, no 'All visitors ashore, please.'

Soon we were chasing down the Clyde after my ship in a very choppy sea, my new uniform getting its first baptism of salty spray. There were more of those days to come. As we caught up with my tanker, I was due another first-time experience, a climb up a rope ladder, a ladder that was swinging from side to side up that aforementioned iron cliffside. 'You'll be OK,' the boatman called after me. That's what I was told throughout the war, but it was hard to believe.

Having achieved the ascent of the steel Everest and reached the deck, I found there was to be no rest yet.

'You're on the bridge, Sparks,' someone called.

'On the bridge?' I queried. 'I'm the radio officer. Shouldn't I be heading for the wireless room?'

'Yes, of course, but you are also the signals officer and on this watch you are on the bridge.'

I climbed up another two companionways (stairs, to the

uninitiated), onto the bridge. I had time to look around at last. We were sailing down the Clyde, Gourock was slipping by and the Cloche Lighthouse was coming up on the port bow. We were approaching the boom defence, a system of iron nets stretched across the river to shut out enemy submarines.

'They are calling you from the boom ship,' the deck officer informed me, putting an Aldis signalling lamp into my hand. I can honestly say that I had never seen this gadget before in my life. Here was another first. But to my relief the Morse code for lamp signalling was very slow, and so I passed muster as lamp signalling officer!

My day of firsts was not over yet. I discovered that the signals officer had also to be proficient in handling flag signals. These were international code flags and pennants that were flown from the masts. Just what had I got myself into? Why hadn't I been instructed in all this? There was one thing for certain: I couldn't pack up and go home. I hastily borrowed a diary from one of the young officer cadets and genned up on the international code flags. Marconi and Samuel Morse had got it together on wireless communication, but they hadn't had to learn flags as well.

There was indeed a skill in handling flags. I found out that flags could be hoisted upside down; there was a top and bottom to each of them. Would you know when a Union flag was upside down? Perhaps *you* would. But *I* didn't. In North Atlantic gales, which were frequent, there were problems. One memorable day the wind tore a hoist of seven flags out of my grasp as I tried to pull them up. They flew straight over the sea and the jumper stay between the two masts had to be let down to retrieve them. The skipper had a lot to say to me in harsh language that I didn't understand, but I knew what he meant.

I learnt that the code flag 'H' meant that we had a pilot on board. The 'Y' meant that we were carrying mail. The 'B' flag, a red flag, indicated that the cargo we were carrying was dangerous. It was under the 'B' flag that our tanker was sailing. Beneath us were twelve thousand tons of aviation fuel for our valiant Air Force. On warm days as we cut through Caribbean seas, we would sit up on the fo'c'sle deck, watching the bows plough the green water, and sing our theme song accompanied by a mouth organ. It was, as you might guess, 'I don't want to set the world on fire.'

After that first trip to the West Indies we returned to Belfast. We had only one day ashore, and I had hoped to be home for Christmas, but no such luck. It was about twenty days for the voyage and twenty hours to load or unload cargo and get back to sea. That was our usual 'turn around' time.

It was just after Christmas Day that we set sail for Curaçao again. Our sister ship went ahead of us, skippered by our captain's brother, both of us heading out to rendezvous with a convoy which was coming up from Liverpool.

I was up on the bridge watching for signals that could be coming to us from the convoy we would be joining. Suddenly there was a mighty flash, followed by the sound of an explosion. Ahead of us, where our sister ship had been a moment before, there was a dense brown cloud of smoke. We hurried to the spot, but when we reached into the clearing smoke there was nothing! Not even a piece of wreckage to be seen. A torpedo had slammed into her, and although she was empty of petrol she had still been full of petroleum gas, a bomb waiting to be touched off. Yes, we were sailing under the 'B' flag and well we knew it! It was a sad Christmas for us all as we journeyed back across the treacherous Atlantic Ocean.

That other world, that world of stark reality, began to make this seventeen-year-old lad begin to re-evaluate life. There was time to think during a four-hour stint on the bridge from midnight till four in the morning. I had been bored at home where nothing ever happened. What was I losing from leaving it? One thing I was very much aware of: there were some things missing aboard ship. When I come to think about it, I don't think I heard anyone say to me, 'Welcome aboard, son.' With all these men aboard I was yet strangely alone in that strange world.

They were frightening days, those early days. 'No need for laxatives here,' they would say and laugh. All the time I was trying hard to learn in order just to survive.

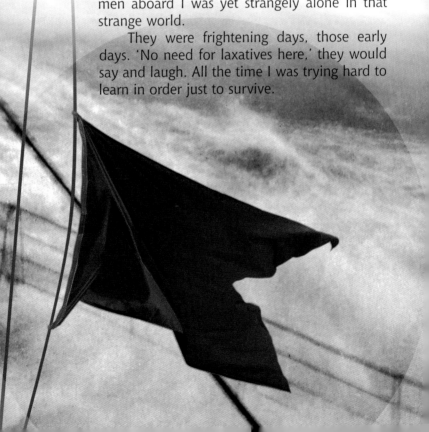

Chapter 3

Through fire and water

During the long night watches, sometimes pacing the bridge to keep warm, sometimes sheltering from the unfriendly elements, I spent my time thinking about home. I had been eager to leave it, but the memory of it wouldn't leave me. Good things are hard to forget. What was it that made it home? Why did I wish I was back there again? Was it the comforts I missed? Those, of course, were sadly missing, but, no, it wasn't things that I had left behind that I missed. Home isn't just a place. Home, I realised, is friends and loved ones.

I thought of those old friends and wondered if they would be thinking of me. They say 'out of sight out of mind', but it wasn't that way with me. My mind would see some of those friends who had met and befriended me and left their mark on my life.

There was one in particular. Maggie Jack her name was. She was a funny old-fashioned lady with wire-rimmed glasses perched on the end of her nose. She was fond of me and embarrassed me no end by coming up to me in the street and giving me a kiss in front of my mates. It meant, if I saw her first, a quick detour or a dash up a side street.

Some said that Maggie was simple. It is true that she

hadn't had much schooling, but I knew she could read. She had only one book in her house. She used to read it to me. It was her Bible, and she had read that book from cover to cover many times over.

One Sabbath day she arrived at church all out of breath. Like the rest of us, she had to climb two flights of stairs to our 'upper room' meeting place. But it was her great excitement that made her out of breath. She had some marvellous thing to tell. At last she came out with it. 'Pigs can swim!' she gasped. Then it was our turn to gasp. 'Yes! Yes! Pigs can really swim!' she almost shouted, and it was a joyous shout.

Let me explain. It was a superstition believed by the old folks that if pigs were thrown into water they didn't try to swim but drowned. It was believed that if they tried to swim they would cut their throats with their trotters.

Maggie lived very close to the shore, and the previous night a very high spring tide had flooded her house. She had come down from her upstairs bedroom just in time to see her kitchen furniture floating out through the doorway and her table and chairs setting out on a sea journey down the Forth. Her next door neighbour's pigs were also flooded out of their sty and, to Maggie's delight, had swum safely to dry land.

'Isn't God a wonderful God!' she exclaimed, 'He saved those poor pigs. He is so good and kind to us!'

She hadn't had any breakfast that morning. No table to set it on. But she could only see a God of love and a God who saved her. Maggie has long gone, but I still think of her. When I remember her, the words of a simple hymn come to mind, 'What a friend we have in Jesus'.

Some time later Maggie found herself a new home. It was a flat above a joiner's shop and yard, sited at the top of a hilly street called Coal Wynd. One day she was shopping in the High Street when someone came rushing up to her, shouting, 'Maggie, Maggie, your house is on fire!'

Maggie turned on her heel and made as fast as her wee body could take her back up the high street and up Coal Wynd. There was a crowd gathering at the top of the street. She pushed through, although some hands tried to prevent her. Through the smoke she could see that all that was left of her home were the two gable ends standing on either side of a heap of smouldering embers. The house and the yard were gutted completely.

Some kind neighbour took Maggie home for the night. Early the next morning she was back again at the site of the tragedy. She stood looking up to where her fireplace had been, one storey up on the gable end of the house. She called to the joiner who was also there, viewing the remains of his business premises.

'Could you please get a ladder and go up and fetch my Bible for me?' she pleaded.

'Get your Bible, Maggie?' the joiner retorted in disbelief. 'Don't be daft, Maggie; there's nothing left in the house, let alone your Bible. It will be burnt to ashes.'

'But it's there, in that wee cupboard by the fireplace,' she maintained with such certainty.

To please the old soul a ladder was fetched. The cupboard door was burnt black and completely carbonised. With a slight knock it crumbled to pieces, but, yes, Maggie's Bible was there, intact; and to crown the miracle, for a miracle it was, on top of the Bible lay a box of 'BlueBell' matches!

I've seen that Bible and smelt its smoky pages, and have seen the box of matches, too. God had answered a simple soul's prayer. Maggie often told people of the wonderful

God who had brought her safely through the fire and water, and they were deeply moved by her childlike faith. None was so moved as I was.

During those long night watches, alone on my part of the ship's bridge with my thoughts to myself, I was to remember Maggie Jack. Once I had laughed at her, along with the others, but at last I began to realise she had something that I hadn't, something that made her happy and free from fear, no matter what happened.

Chapter 4

The little blue Bible

Mum was hovering over me as I packed my suit-case. I was off on another trip after a few days' leave at home. I could see that she wanted to ask me something.

'Why don't you take your Bible with you?' she said, half hesitatingly. She knew that I wasn't showing much interest in the church now that I had found a new life and had left her care.

I replied as kindly as I could, 'Well, not this time, Mum.' I didn't want my mates to see me with a Bible among my gear. After all, I was a big boy now!

It had been years since I had received that little Blue Bible as a prize at a Boys' Brigade Bible class. It had an anchor embossed on the cover and the BB motto, 'Sure and steadfast', written in gold letters across the anchor. Mum thought it would be very appropriate to take it to sea with its anchor and all. I hurriedly changed the subject of Bibles and went on to fetch other things to pack. Out of the corner of my eye, I saw Mum slip the Bible under some of the clothes in the suitcase. Of course I said nothing, for I didn't want to hurt her feelings nor her expectations of me.

I remember receiving that prize. It was awarded to me

for being able to write out all the books of the Bible in correct order and correctly spelled. I remember also that I had difficulty in spelling the book Habakkuk.

It was old Maggie Jack who had come to my rescue. I laugh now when I hear her saying to me, 'This is how to spell it. It goes like this – an H and an A and a B and an A and a K and a K and a U and a K.' She repeated this with a kind of beat in her voice.

I had hoped the award was going to be one of those large boys' books, and I was disappointed on prize day when I was handed a little blue Bible instead.

After all those years it seemed that I was still ashamed of possessing it, as back aboard ship when unpacking my luggage I was careful to hide it right at the bottom of one of my drawers.

The first part of the voyage was uneventful, just the normal routines of a North Atlantic convoy. As usual, after many days at sea, the secret was revealed, our destination. It was to be Quebec.

There we loaded a cargo of bulk grain and I genned up on the Canadian seaport. I liked to know about the places we visited. I had read about General James Wolfe and saw the Heights of Abraham that he stormed one night. After a fifteen-minute battle he defeated the French general Montcalm, taking Canada for the British. Both generals were mortally wounded. What a waste of good men war is.

In no time we were off again down the great St Lawrence River and out into the Atlantic past Belle Island. On this island there was an important radio station that furnished us with special weather reports, and in particular the location of moving icebergs. The danger on that occasion was not to be the menace of ice, however, but the fury of the Atlantic gales. The wind plays havoc with the sea, especially if it is a cyclonic wind.

Before long on our journey eastwards we found ourselves being driven by a following wind and a following sea. The barometer was falling rapidly. It soon became impossible to keep convoy stations safely, and so it was every ship for herself. Great mountains of sea began crashing down on our stern. There was no way we could turn our ship around to head into the storm, for we would have certainly capsized. Our heavily laden vessel was floundering around like a cork, uncontrollable and unsteerable.

I was afraid, to say the least, really scared. Here was a fear that was something more than the fear I had for lurking submarines. The sheer helplessness of being at the mercy of the howling, screaming wind and the great menacing mountains of sea, topped with rollers that crashed down on to our wallowing vessel, was the fear of all fears for poor inexperienced me. One minute we were on the top of the mountain of sea, taking the full force of the hurricane wind; the next moment we were diving down into the dark trough of the boiling ocean

It was hard clinging to the rails as we moved around the ship. It was difficult to keep a footing anywhere as we twisted, and heaved, and battled to keep upright. The deck officer pointed out to me the alarming situation we were in. The tarpaulin over the hatch covers was being ripped off by the wind and the sea that we were heavily shipping. Should the sea water break into the hold and into the grain cargo, there would be an even greater danger – the danger of the grain being soaked, and swelling, and bursting the internal bulkheads. What would happen next we didn't know.

At my off duty time I stumbled down to my cabin on

the main deck. Water was swilling back and forth on my cabin floor so, dead tired, I swung myself up onto my bunk to keep my feet dry and try to have some rest. But there was no resting for me, neither physically nor mentally. I keep saying this, but when I look back to that awful time I was absolutely afraid. Was that to be my end, a watery grave?

I lit a cigarette, the usual comfort, but there was no comfort in a cigarette that time. I really don't know why, perhaps it was a last resort to find peace of mind, but I reached down into my drawer beside my bunk and fished around and found the little blue Bible.

I didn't know where to open it to. It's true that I had learned to memorise and to spell all the books in it, but really all I knew then was that it was God's book and that others believed it with all their hearts. I had seen the comfort and assurance it had given to some of those old folks at home.

Mum kept hers always near her. It was old and tatty from much use. The text was underlined here and there, and all through it there were scribbled notes and comments. She used to tell me she would never change it for a new one. Why wouldn't she change it? I often wondered. Later I was to learn that some of those stains were tear stains; some of them had fallen on it as she prayed for me.

Having taken the wee Bible in my hand, I was quick to throw the cigarette that was in the other hand down into the water swilling around the deck under my bunk. I can see it now being extinguished and floating away. I then opened the little Book and began at first just to look. It was open at the book called Isaiah. I turned the pages back to the first chapter, thinking it best to begin at the beginning of the book. I read on, not fully understanding what I read, till something that I could clearly understand made me stop and read it again. It was there in verse 18 of that first chapter of Isaiah.

'Come, now, and let us reason together, saith the Lord: though your sins be as scarlet, they shall be as white as snow: though they be red like crimson, they shall be as wool.'

It was as if God were saying to me, 'Come on now, lad. Let's talk this out, reasonably, man to man. Yes, you have sinned; I know all about it. You are feeling that you have come to the end of a short life and you are not ready to go. In fact, you feel that you are not only not ready to go but fearful of where you might go with a weight of sin on your shoulders.' I felt that God was saying to *me*, sinful me, 'I can forgive your sins, no matter how crimson they are.'

Here was a precious gift that I didn't deserve, being offered to me freely and directly.

With a full heart I accepted it.

Miracles do happen. A moment before I opened that little blue Bible I had been in deep despair with nothing but the fear of a watery grave for company.

As I sat there on my bunk, still aboard that stricken ship, my burden lifted and the awful fear went. I said a prayer, an unspoken prayer from the heart, to the God who had revealed himself to me. I said thank you to him. Not a 'thank you' for being about to save me from the sea, for we were yet far from safety.

The paramount thing from that moment was that I had found a Saviour and it really didn't matter what happened from then on.

Later, back again on the bridge, another miracle happened; at least I thought it was a miracle at the time, for my eyes were open to wonderful things happening then. Suddenly the wind ceased. The howling and screaming stopped. For a moment I thought God was saying, 'Peace, be still', just for me! But the chief officer shattered my illusion. 'No, Sparks,' he said, 'the storm is not over by far. You see, we have just run into the eye of the hurricane. When we pass through it we shall run into the storm at the other side of the eye, which will be coming from the other direction.'

And so we did, just as he said, but we survived.

And so it was with me, too. There were to be stormy times yet to come and pass, and calms amid the storms. Now avidly reading that little blue Bible, I was to discover that I was not the only one to encounter frightful storms at sea. I read Psalm 107 and found a description of the self-same experience that I had had. The writer must surely have sailed through the eye of a hurricane, too. Here are his words and mine. You will find them in Psalm 107 verses 23 to 32:

PSALM 107.23

23 Some went down to the sea in
   ships,
   doing business on the mighty
   waters;
24 they saw the deeds of the LORD,
   his wondrous works in the
   deep.
25 For he commanded and raised the
   stormy wind,
   which lifted up the waves of the
   sea.
26 They mounted up to heaven, they
   went down to the depths;
   their courage melted away in
   their calamity;
27 they reeled and staggered like
   drunkards,
   and were at their wits' end.

28 Then they cried to the LORD in
   their trouble,
   and he brought them out from
   their distress;
29 he made the storm be still,
   and the waves of the sea were
   hushed.
30 Then they were glad because they
   had quiet,
   and he brought them to their
   desired haven.
31 Let them thank the LORD for his
   steadfast love,
   for his wonderful works to
   humankind.
32 Let them extol him in the
   congregation of the people,
   and praise him in the assembly
   of the elders.

Chapter 5

Leviathans

It was Alfred, Lord Tennyson who wrote, 'I heard time flowing in the middle of the night, and all things floating to a day of doom.'

In the war at sea it was also true that many things floated to their doom and gloom. There were sunny days and happy days and, for me, things of wonder to see. First, it was meeting the ships, especially the big ships.

Somehow, I believe that the Bible Psalmist must surely have been down to the sea himself, a long time before me, because he says in Psalm 104 verse 26, 'There go the ships: there is that leviathan, whom thou hast made to play therein.'

There go the ships indeed, the big ships, the really big ocean liners. I saw them and wondered at their size. There they were, painted in their wartime grey colour, besmudged with camouflage. It made them appear like great mythological creatures from another world, moving over the seas.

On the River Clyde I well remember how they elbowed one another for a place to anchor. What a busy river it was in those days! Troopships, warships and merchantmen coming and going furtively night and day. On the river banks the shipyards echoed with the sound of riveting.

Amid sparks and smoke and flashes of miniature light-
ning new vessels were being born on the slipways. But my
eyes were on the troopships majestically waiting for their
cargoes of men.

I can still see the Polish liners, the *Pilsudski* and the
Batorea, and that strange French ship the *Louis Pasteur* with
her singularly tall funnel that seemed too big for her; but
what did I know about ship design?

In those days it was the many-funnelled liners that were
all the rage. Funnels spoke speed, and the more funnels the
more esteem the ship had. The old *Acquitania* sported four
of these prestigious smoke stacks. Years later when I took
my bride Joy back to see the sights of Bonnie Scotland
we had the last sighting of that grand old lady of the sea.
On a trip up the sea loch called Gareloch we saw the
Acquitania being scrapped, her dignity disintegrating into a
sad heap of scrap metal.

But I had the privilege of seeing them in their heyday –
the fabulous RMS *Queen Mary* speeding out of New York
harbour, passing us as we laboured out, as if we were
standing still, that monster of 81,235 tons, and her sister,
the *Queen Elizabeth* of 83,673 tons; the largest liners in the
world at that time.

Once we lay at anchor beside the *Empress of Japan* in
Gibraltar. Later when the Japanese nation turned out to be
our enemy, the ship's name was changed to the *Empress of
Scotland*. I think that suited her better.

In Capetown, South Africa, we anchored beside some
of the great men of war; the awe-inspiring battleships, the
Rodney, the *Repulse*, the *Prince of Wales* and the *Duke
of York*. I will tell you of a meeting we had with this last-
mentioned battleship in a later chapter. We socialised
ashore with the lads from these ships and it was personally

tragic news for me when we heard some time later of the loss of the *Rodney* and the *Repulse* in the Indian Ocean.

Yes, I've had close contact with the mightiest of them all, His Majesty's Ship the *Hood*, and again it was a mighty blow to hear of her sinking by the German pocket battleship the *Bismark*. Even the mightiest fell. What a dreadful war it was at sea, and what loss of life! The Mercantile Marine, to which I belonged, suffered as well as the Royal Navy. Perhaps it is not generally known but it suffered more loss of lives than any of the other services, Army, Navy or Air Force. One in every four merchant sailors never came home again. Our name was changed and elevated from Mercantile Marine to the Merchant Navy.

Returning to the spectacle of the big ships, perhaps I understood in a special way how big they were. I could, with experience, compare their size with a small merchantman that I sailed on. She was called the *Ary Lensen*, a Norwegian ship, and she was only around a thousand tons. Recently I was researching into ancient ships that plied the Mediterranean Sea in Bible times, and I was amazed to find that the ship that sailed out of Alexandria and picked up the apostle Paul was possibly around twelve hundred tons – bigger than the *Ary Lensen*. Now I understand the plight Paul was in during the Bible recorded shipwreck that happened off the northern coast of Malta. A wee ship in a heavy sea, climbing up one side of a wave and down the other side. So it was with us in the unfriendly Atlantic Ocean in wintertime.

But continuing with the theme of Leviathans, I once had a strange experience out there in that lonely Atlantic Ocean. We were sailing home over a tranquil ocean, a 'flat calm'. It was just after 4 am. I had completed the midnight watch, and as I left the wireless room, not really feeling like sleep, I decided not to retire to my cabin which was on the boat deck, but climbed down onto the main deck for a little stroll. The ship was a petrol tanker, and with a full load she sailed very low in the water. Perhaps there would be only two metres of freeboard above the sea. It was such a beautiful, peaceful night, and the stars above were twinkling so brightly – as they do at sea far away from the polluted atmosphere above land.

As I walked the deck, deep in thought, I could hear only the swish of the sea as it ran past the side of the ship. I walked on forward, away from the midship accommodation and out towards the bow of the ship. It's good to look over the bow and watch the stem cutting through the water. Suddenly I had a strange feeling that I was not alone. I was sure that there was no one else on the deck at that unearthly time, yet I felt as if someone was looking at me. Then over my shoulder, from the sea, I heard a faint movement of water being pushed aside and, turning round, I found myself looking into the eye of a monster. Eyeball to eyeball with a great whale gliding so softly alongside the ship, keeping equal pace with us, a great black hulk, shining in the bright moonlight.

The whale looked at me, his eye so human-like. What did he think about as he looked at me and I looked at him? An acknowledgement seemed to pass between us, and after what seemed to be an incredible length of time he silently picked up speed and moved on before us. I saw him submerge into the blackness of the night sea, and suddenly he was gone with a great splash of his mammoth tail.

May I refer you to that text of Scripture I mentioned before, from Psalm 104 verse 26? The Psalmist exclaimed, 'There go the ships', but notice that in the same breath he also added with glee, 'There is that leviathan, whom thou hast made to play therein.' Wasn't he really meaning both the ships and the whale?

Was that great whale playing with me that night? Was he looking for me to play with him, like the friendly dolphins and happy porpoises that so often play around our ships for hours, following us and diving under our bows? They are God's lovely creatures and I know he created them to be our friends.

That was the night I met the great leviathan of the deep, whose ancestors survived the Flood of Noah's day. There was obviously no room in the Ark for them, but thanks to a wonderful God they survived the Flood and its worldwide devastation.

I have often thought of that whale since and asked myself, Where is he now? I too, like him in a way, became a survivor in those troubled waters of World War Two. I have never really been very good at anything I have done in life, but there is one thing I have been fairly good at and that is surviving. The survival hasn't been down to my skill and prowess but entirely down to a loving God. I'll be telling you what he did for me.

Chapter 6

Friday the thirteenth

It was March 1942; wintry, cold and bleak. I had joined the MV *Rothley*, my new ship. The night before, falling over railway lines in the dark and gloom of the blackout on Salford docks, I had found her with difficulty.

That day we were sailing down the thirty-two miles of the Manchester Ship Canal, down towards the Mersey estuary, bound for where we didn't know.

It was strange, looking out from the ship's portholes and seeing fields and farmhouses going by. In one field by the canal schoolboys were playing football. They could quite easily have kicked their ball right onto our deck.

My uncelebrated birthday had just passed me by and the day was the thirteenth and a Friday. I remember this only too well for some of my superstitious mates kept saying to each other, 'This is Friday and it's the thirteenth; we'll never bring her back,' and would you believe it, superstition or not, we never did bring her back.

We arrived at Runcorn and tied up for the night under Runcorn Bridge. There we were to await our call to join the next convoy. That evening we went ashore in the pouring rain, just to escape the grey old ship for a brief spell of freedom. We came back aboard cold and wet and with an awesome hunger. One of our gang mentioned that he had seen a great pile of peeled potatoes in the galley and suggested that we make ourselves some chips. That we did with relish, and what glorious chips they were!

Thinking about that pile of peeled potatoes takes me to another thought. I remember a crew member who swaggered around the ship on sunny days showing off his bared muscles and sporting all over his arms, chest, and even his back, such an array of tattoos, the like of which I had never seen before. I tried to guess what job this 'Hercules' had aboard ship. Guess what? He was the galley boy! It was he who had spent most of the day peeling those potatoes. It takes a lot of spuds to feed forty-two men who ate them with each of the three meals a day.

The *Rothley* was a happy ship. The crew were mostly Geordies from Newcastle upon Tyne, rough but easygoing. Soon we were off to spend the next month at sea, leaving the cold and rain behind us. For those next four weeks we never as much as caught sight of land anywhere, until we put our bows under the shelter of Table Mountain in Capetown, South Africa. There we found out the reason for our voyage. Everything was meant to be a great mystery to confuse the Nazis, but it was just as much a source of confusion to us! Apparently we had been sent from England with a shipload of munitions to support the invasion of Madagascar, off the coast of Africa, but we had been too long getting there, dodging submarines for four weeks back and forth, across and down the Atlantic. Consequently, the invasion of Madagascar went on without us. After a few days we were sent off again with our lethal cargo, as far away as possible, to far-off Bombay. It looked as we were being punished for being bad boys.

The Indian Ocean is the setting for my next two stories. We were sailing out of convoy all by ourselves, and my duties confined me almost entirely to the wireless room for eight hours a day. It was a pity to miss all the lovely sunshine I could have been enjoying on the bridge, but there was much excitement yet to come.

One morning I was alerted by the speaking-tube whistle. This ingenious device was used aboard ship to communicate with the bridge, engine room and wireless room. It was just a tube with a whistle stuck in either end through which you blew and spoke. Nobody seems to have been credited with its invention. I could well imagine that the ancient Egyptians or Romans had it aboard their galleys.

'Sparks, could you come up to the bridge?' I was summoned by the Third Officer, who added, 'Bring your signalling lamp with you.' Another ship had been spotted sailing just under the horizon. After a time it had altered its course and was now sailing towards us. Rumour was, that it could be a 'Q Ship', a disguised armed raider, a merchantman with guns concealed in its holds.

The ship was coming within signalling distance and I was asked to call her up. She made no reply. I tried several times but our 'friends' remained silent, although it was obvious that they could see my lamp signals and we could see them plainly on their bridge. Alarmed, the captain ordered the DEMS gun crew to load and stand by our 4.7 inch JAP gun mounted on our stern.

As she was coming abeam of us, again I heard the 'Old Man' order one of our cadets to run up the 'Red Duster', our British Merchant Navy flag. That moment I shall never forget. It was the moment of truth. We were telling them bravely who we were, but could only ask who they were. Our eyes were glued upon the mystery ship. Ready to commence battle with our one little gun, we turned to port, bringing our stern around, preparing to shoot.

There was a deathly silence; only the sound of the sea could be heard. Without a word, without a signal of acknowledgement, she passed on by. Ships that pass in the night they say; that one passed in broad daylight. We never did find out who she was.

The encounter somehow shook us out of our complacency. We came to realise that we weren't there for a cruise. It was decided that we had better brush up on our gunnery. Our gun had never really been fired. For practice, a float was dropped overboard and when it was far enough astern the gun crew began firing, using live shells. All had gone well for a short time; the entire crew were on deck enjoying the novelty event, then the target practice suddenly came to an end. There had been a misfire of some kind and dutifully the gun breach was left closed and no tampering was attempted, for there was a live shell still in the gun. The entertainment was over and we went on our way.

Days later we approached Bombay harbour and were met by the usual navy defence corvette that policed the entrance to the harbour. I was on the bridge talking with my signal lamp to the corvette and answering the customary questions for ship identification. The captain interrupted me and casually said, 'You'd better tell them about the gun that didn't go off.' Moments later I was aware of a commotion going on aboard the corvette, followed by a signal from her which read, 'Turn about and put to sea.' Turn about and put to sea?

We were being thrown out of Bombay harbour, post haste! According to them we had a ticking time bomb aboard our ship, an unexploded shell on a ship loaded with ammunition.

It's so funny to think back. There we had been, sleeping

peacefully in our bunks every night since our target-practice day, with never a thought of danger.

The experts came aboard when we were well away from the shipping lane. They moved all of us crew to the other end of the ship and hosed the gun down with gallons of water and, finally, after a long tense interval they opened the breach of the gun and removed the trouble, a faulty charge. They replaced the charge and fired off the shell that had been sitting in there all those days.

Soon we 'lepers' were accepted back into the harbour; everything was shipshape and safe. Did I say 'safe'? A few days later, when our lethal cargo was unloaded from our hold – bombs, shells and detonators – some of that lethal cargo was actually dropped from the crane slings as they were swung ashore and bounced on the quay. I tell you, we were so relieved to leave Bombay docks and head out again into the safe Indian Ocean.

We were now an empty ship looking for a cargo. The powers that be decided to route us back over the Indian Ocean to Africa, to Mombasa. There we encountered another enemy we didn't expect, the most unfriendly mosquitoes on earth!

There was nothing there for us except a part cargo bound for Durban, South Africa, and it was not the nicest cargo, either, for it was infested with gigantic spiders. They found their way all around the ship, including the cabins.

Once again there was nothing for us in Durban when we arrived there, so we were soon off again to continue our 'Tramping'. We rounded the Cape of Good Hope and were given a destination – Port of Spain, Trinidad.

The voyage that started on Friday the thirteenth was about to reach its fateful destination and we the crew would, as naval jargon goes, be 'Discharged at Sea', says my Merchant Navy Discharge Book.

It was October and we were back up over the equator and a few hundred miles short of Trinidad.

At three in the morning all was deathly quiet inside my stuffy wireless room. Outside was the sea, and beyond, more sea and the darkness of a moonless night. It had been a long, monotonous trip from South Africa. Our destination, Trinidad, was too far away for us to be counting the days till our arrival. It was unbearably hot in the confined wireless room. Did I say wire*less* room? It was literally crammed *full* of wires. Wires connecting switches of every kind, battery-charging boards, with glowing lamps, instruments with flickering dials, and aerial wires leading up through the deckhead from receivers and transmitters. If only I could have shut the system down for a time and opened a porthole for some fresh air. But no. As third radio officer it was my penance to sit out the midnight watch, that is, midnight till 4 am. The batteries had to go on charging and cooking the air. The emergency power that they provided had to be there for any immediate emergency, our survival link with the world beyond us.

The heat was overwhelming and it was hard to stay alert. Even my radio receiver seemed to have gone to sleep. It hadn't said anything to me since I came on watch. There were no ships trafficking messages anywhere within radio distance. My log book in front of me was empty, except for the every-fifteen-minute compulsory entry that formed a monotonous column: 'No signals heard'.

Below decks all were asleep, sweltering in their bunks, their electric fans churning hot air around their bare bodies. Even on duty, and since this was a tramp ship with a lower protocol, I was wearing a very brief pair of khaki shorts and my Indian hand-made sandals. Sweat trickled off my elbows and smudged the indelible pencil notations on my log book.

To keep alert I was trying hard to read a book, a not-so-well-known classic novel, Dickens' last, *The Mystery of Edwin Drood*. But I wasn't making much headway with it.

What I am going to relate now is very hard to explain. One moment I was sitting there on my swivel chair, trying to pick up the threads of the story, and the next moment I was lying on the deck with half of my instruments piled up on top of me! My mind was a blank and I just couldn't think what had happened.

When I came into full consciousness, I felt that the old ship had risen up into the air, just as if she had run her sleek bows up and over another ship, or on to a coral reef. Then, just as suddenly, I felt as if she was shaking and shuddering back down again into the sea. The shuddering went on, accompanied by a dull roaring.

The friendly throb of the engines had stopped.

My ears were strangely numb and quite sore. I didn't know this then, but when a 22-inch torpedo explodes just below you, you are too close to the bang to hear it.

All kinds of thoughts ran through my muddled brain. I pulled myself out from amid the wreckage of the wireless room and set out to do what I had to do. I had always dreaded what was now happening, and had wondered if I would cope. Suddenly there was no time to wonder about my inabilities. There was a mess of apparatus around me that needed sorting out, and a distress signal to be sent.

I don't know how long it took, but the emergency transmitter was at last ready for action. I pressed the starter switch and the generator burst into life. But what next? What was I to say to the world outside? What had happened to us? Where were we?

The bridge had not contacted me, so I called the bridge.

There was no reply. I would have to find out for myself. I pushed open the wireless room door, which opened out onto the side of the bridge. I was in for a shock.

What I saw were angry, roaring flames spewing up over the front of the bridge. We had been torpedoed forward of the bridge housing and our fuel tanks were ablaze.

I closed the door against the heat and smoke. I had a job that I had to do, whatever the others were doing. Among the mess on my table I found a piece of paper given to me at the beginning of the watch. On it were our given estimates of our ship's position at every half-hour interval through the watch. It was 3 am and I knew where we were estimated to be, so I commenced sending out a distress signal. Not the SOS of pre-war days, I hasten to add. We had an extremely interesting emergency code that I will tell you about later, now that the period of the secrecy act has terminated.

I could see by my instruments that our aerial had been severed or fouled and little of my message was being radioed. But I persevered slowly and deliberately, for out there maybe there was somebody who just might be near enough to hear our signal.

Then through the wireless room door my chief appeared, dazed and bewildered, just like me. He dutifully took over responsibility.

For a moment I could think of myself, selfishly, perhaps, but only for a moment as it turned out. Suddenly I felt the deck below us angling over onto its side.

Pulling myself from the doorway and looking forward, I could see that the ship was rapidly sinking down by her bows. The stern was rising up behind us, up and up.

Loose objects were rushing down the deck. The jib cranes at the main mast were swinging round wildly. The noise was tremendous as the ship twisted and turned, as if in agony, rearing up from the stern.

I shouted to Bill, my chief, and, unable to stop myself, slid down the afterbridge deck onto the bridge itself. The bridge was submerging and the sea closed around me. She was going under.

All hell broke loose around me – the noise, the crashing, the rending and the choking smoke and heat. For a brief moment the cold sea that embraced me felt so good, but only for a moment.

Suddenly an alarming realisation hit me. I just had to get away from this ship! As far away and as soon as possible. If I didn't, she would take me down with her. I began to swim as I had never swum before. I swam until I was utterly exhausted. Desperately, I turned around in the water to see how far I had distanced myself from the wreck, and saw my stricken ship with her bows and bridge submerged and her stern high up in the sky above me.

Frozen with fear, I watched as the vessel seemed to stand, hesitate for a moment, and then begin her death plunge. I was far, far too near her! Frantically I began to swim from her. I could feel the water under me being sucked back towards her. I was fighting a losing battle to get away. My fear turned to abject terror. This was it! I screamed to God to save me.

Then I was afloat on the surface of the sea with a deathly silence all around me. Above, I could see myriads of stars sparkling in the night sky. I was alive!

I felt hot blood trickling from my nose. My ears felt blasted. Yes, she had taken me down some depth with her but I had come up again. I gulped down that beautiful fresh air. I did it again and again with great relish.

The *Rothley* was gone, sunk by U-boat U-332, and I was alone. The sea around me was calm and almost soundless. Then, in that deathly silence around me, as if echoing back across the sea, I could hear my own pitiful screams to God for help. Screams that just a moment before had been so desperate and full of despair. And there, in the middle of that lonely place in the ocean, I shed a burning tear, a tear of heartfelt shame. God had heard my shouts and, though I had no faith in him, he had saved me.

Back in that fearful time in the eye of the hurricane he had said to me, in my little blue Bible, 'Come let us reason together.' He understood me then and was ready to accept me in all my sins. Now it was my turn to trust him and accept the undeserved love he was giving to me.

The old ship is still down there today in Davy Jones's Locker, a mile or two below the surface of that ill-fated place. It was quite true, as my mates had prophesied; we didn't bring her back, and it was truly a tragedy. The day she sank, 19 October, was a milestone in my life. That night my Saviour and I became real friends, just Jesus and me, miles from anywhere.

By the way, in case you think I've forgotten, the 'emergency code' to which I referred on page 41 went like this. Instead of the usual SOS, we would use SSS if being attacked by a submarine; RRR if attacked by a 'Raider'; and AAA meant that we were being attacked by air. This time-saving code meant that we had no need for further explanation.

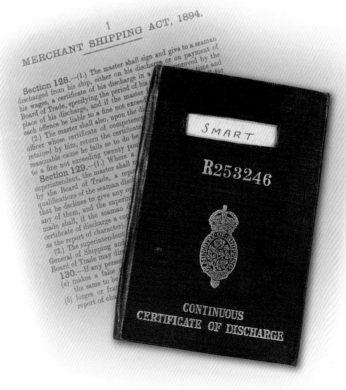

Chapter 7

Discharged at sea

I became a DBS

D o you remember Jonah, the reluctant Bible prophet who descended, quite literally, into the belly of a great fish because he chose not to follow God's instructions to go to Nineveh? His state down there has been described as follows :

Dumped overboard by a crew of a ship, who feared that they would be sunk in the storm because of Jonah's sin against his God, he found himself *down* in the stomach of the leviathan, very much *down* in the mouth, so to speak, and now *down* at the bottom of the sea. Just how far down could *I* have gone the day of our sinking? And there was still another unexpected down' to come that night.

Floating there on the surface, I thought at first that I was all alone. But soon, by the light of the stars, I found others swimming beside me. Some were clutching floating bits of wreckage, and others farther from us were calling out to one another. Later, when we got together, and were consoling ourselves with our miraculous escapes, the atmosphere of relief suddenly changed dramatically to one of dread again.

Out of the darkness, without warning, a blinding light suddenly stabbed at us. Behind the searchlight loomed the great black hulk of the submarine that had torpedoed us.

It was a German U-boat and she was coming towards us to check her kill and count her victims. From her deck came a burst of machine-gun fire, and a harsh voice called out, 'Whaat sheep was eet?'

Fearing another hail of bullets, someone promptly shouted back from the sea below her, 'The *Rothley*'. The reply was another burst of fire directed straight at us, cowering in the water. The voice, much angrier than at first, came back, 'Whaat? The *Rodney*?' It became frighteningly apparent that the German officer thought we were trying to fool him, for the *Rodney*, as you may know, was one of the great capital ships in our navy. You could put this down to like-sounding words being confused, but it was no fun for us at the wrong end of the gun! We made haste to correct the misunderstanding, and to our relief the searchlight was extinguished and the submarine silently disappeared into the darkness of the night.

We were left to survive as best we could. It looked like a hopeless situation, for no one had been able to launch a lifeboat from the sinking ship. But daylight came at last, after a seemingly endless night and a long, long swim.

There was a shout. Someone had found a partly-submerged small boat that had floated away from the ship as she sank. We swam to it and began to bail it out with one bailer and lots of eagerly cupped hands. We thanked God that it was a calm sea. The boat would to be our home, all 42 of us, for the next week.

It was a bit cramped, with seats available only for those manning the oars. The freeboard of the boat was only a few inches above sea level, and with the least of waves the water tumbled in over the sides, necessitating continuous bailing out. We all took turns. We had only one beaker or little barrel of fresh water and no food at all. Oh, yes, there was a pack of Horlicks sweets, but in one rationing we ate the lot, paper wrappings and all.

Of the twenty-seven million tons of shipping that we had at the outset of the war, by 1942 fourteen million tons lay at the bottom of the ocean. There were lots of survivors like us with no ship. We earned the distinguished title of DBS, which meant Distressed British Seamen. On that memorable day in October 1942 I became a DBS.

I later found out that to become a DBS was rather like the state in which Jonah found himself – despised and very much 'downed'. I discovered, too, that on that fateful day, as if it were my fault for losing my ship, my salary was terminated and I was 'on the dole'! From then on I had become, in some people's estimation, a scrounger on National Benefit. There were more down sides yet to come, but back to my story.

Things were rough aboard the lifeboat. Strangely, though, I was aware that my fear had gone. Somehow I knew that all would be well. Just knowing that all would be well meant that I was trusting in my new-found Friend. I realised that trusting him was really what faith was all about and I had found it.

Rough as it was, tossing around in that open boat, even DBSs found time to have a laugh. Let me tell you about one of those moments.

It had all started weeks before, aboard ship. Jack, my mate, being an artist by profession, had begun illustrating our shipboard news-sheet. We called it 'The Daily Liar' for obvious reasons. The news it contained was very much a fabrication. Jack would insert a cartoon of one of our noted crew members. One day it was a portrait of our chief engineer. He was a tall, dour, thin-faced individual, not given to much smiling. His caricature emphasised the rather large ears he had been blessed with. And so there he was, an egg-shaped circle for his head with two very large circles on either side for his ears. Everywhere you went around the ship, someone had chalked this symbol of the chief, a small circle with two large circles either side. The chief, needless to say, was furious.

On board our ship we also had a pet monkey. Well, maybe not so much a pet, for it was given to thieving, and spent most of its time escaping up the mast from its many pursuers who were longing to get their hands on it.

Like us, the monkey had become a DBS, and found itself, with us, in a lifeboat. The poor creature became very thirsty and began drinking the sea water, for our water was far too precious and scant to share with the monkey. It became quite crazed, and in its madness began to dash among us. It bit some of us. I wonder if you can guess who got bitten first? You've got it, the chief engineer. And guess again, where do you think it bit him? Right again, his ear! Well, even he had to crack a smile, poor soul.

The long monotonous days were spent crouching down in the boat, trying to avoid the burning sun during the day and the coldness of the seemingly longer nights. We had given up trying to row the boat anywhere. The sail we rigged had been ripped in a sudden squall, so we just floated aimlessly with the sea.

One day a lone cloud brought a shower of rain upon us. We hastily spread out the tatters of the sail to try to catch some of this liquid gold. We did manage to trap a quantity but had no cup or jug to empty it into. One of our engineer greasers offered us his boots that he had hung onto. We filled them up and passed them round like a holy grail. The liquid was wet but not very refreshing!

Nearly every day someone thought that he saw a ship on the horizon. Now and again a wave could look like a distant vessel. Wishful thinking can play tricks on your imagination. As we crouched together, half sleeping, half dreaming, I thought I heard someone call out, 'Oh, come on, give me a bit of your orange, mate.' We all instantly roused ourselves out of our stupor and looked around to see who had been hiding an orange. There was no orange. It was just one poor lad who had become deranged and was voicing his imaginings. I wish I could have given him a bite of that delicious orange he was dreaming about.

Then one day someone called out again, 'There's a ship!' But no one was in a mood of expectancy. Even I didn't respond very quickly. I was just very tired and very sleepy. I became aware that some of the lads were talking and the talk grew louder. Almost reluctantly I looked up and, yes, there was a ship!

The sea was quite stormy. One moment our little boat was riding on top of the swell. The next, it was down at the bottom of a watery valley. From the top of each wave we could clearly see a ship, a tanker, abeam of us.

Frantically we fished a smoke flare from the boat's locker. When ignited, it gave off a dense red smoke that curled up into the air above us. We watched the ship to see if she would notice our signal. After an eternity she did see it, altering her course towards us. A spontaneous cheer rose from each of our parched throats; suddenly we were wide awake and our hearts beat again.

Manoeuvring alongside us, the tanker, which turned out to be Spanish, brought us to her leeside. Thus she sheltered us from the heavy waves that were bobbing our little craft ten or twelve feet up and down her side. A rope ladder was flung over the tanker's side and I, being the youngest survivor, was ordered to mount it first. Waiting till our boat was on top of a swell, I grabbed the ladder with both hands. My arms were strong and eager in my excitement to pull myself up on the ladder to safety at last. But my legs failed me. The long time sitting with my feet constantly in water had weakened my lower limbs. Clinging to the ladder, I was fearful that I would still be hanging there helplessly on the first rung when the next wave brought the boat crashing upward again! At last, amid my panic and fear, I felt two strong arms embrace me, pulling me up to safety. One of the big Spanish sailors had come to my rescue. They could have been the arms of Jesus! Maybe they were, really. Indeed, he was there, in it all, as I had known he would be.

At last we were all safe, lying there on the warm, dry, sunny deck of that Spanish tanker. I think we were all counting our blessings. I did more than most.

Our hosts gave us little to eat at first, but lots to drink. Empty stomachs don't take too kindly to a sudden influx of food, and our friends knew this all too well.

The Spaniards were poor lads, but at that moment we were poorer still. None of us was fully clothed, and the scant clothes we had on when we were torpedoed were stinking with fuel oil. The oil that we swam through to escape the burning ship had impregnated everything about us and had become baked on our skin while we'd been exposed in the lifeboat. I had only my shorts on, and we had picked up the chief officer wearing only his cap! The kind Spaniards shared their clothes with us.

I fell heir to a pair of pyjama bottoms that had obviously belonged to a very corpulent gentleman, and in order to make them stay up I knotted them tightly at the waist. Fine, until we arrived at our destination, the island of Aruba. There they became a big embarrassment to me.

The British Consul on the island was duly informed of our arrival and our predicament, particularly our need of clothing. He had no time to be personally involved with DBSs and their problems, so sent a message back to the ship for us to report to him at the consulate uptown. I can still see us now, trooping along the dockside, a motley crowd of clowns bedecked in strange garments.

There was I, clutching my pyjama bottoms, as we took that shame-filled march along the main street of Orangestad, seeing only the cracks in the pavements and praying that we would be invisible to the onlookers.

So there it was for us poor torpedoed sailors – a memorable lesson in humility. A 'downer' that I really don't think we deserved. Yet for me, beyond that awful moment, there was another chance to make a success of my life, and a new hope was being born within me.

Chapter 8

'England expects'

The next few voyages took me back again to the cold grey seas of the North Atlantic and back to the notorious Atlantic convoys. The German U-boat fleet was increasing rapidly as Hitler made a bid to starve Britain into a 'siege surrender'. Every merchant ship was a vital link in our survival in those dark days. Our armies had been driven off the continent of Europe, and on our island we were fighting for our very existence.

As the U-boat numbers increased so did the attacks on our ships. It was a constant battle to keep up the incoming supplies as more and more of our ships, along with their cargoes, went down in the Atlantic. Naval escort ships were being taxed to their utmost as they endeavoured to protect larger and larger convoys.

At this time in my story the winter weather was at its worst, adding yet further dangers to our passage from the United States. But even the dreadful weather did not deter the U-boats in their attacks.

Doing the deck watch one morning, I was cold and wet and miserable on the exposed wing of the bridge. Four hours is a long time to be buffeted by wind and rain and blown spume from the rough seas. 'Dutifully', that's the word that overrules all personal wishes in this man's navy.

I was keeping my eye on the commodore ship directing the convoy and its naval escorts. The messages were passed from the commodore down along the lines of the ships in the convoy. Alterations to course and speed could come at any time as we zigzagged in an attempt to foil the submarine attacks which, in turn, could also come at any time. We had been into our voyage only a few days and already some of the convoy had been sunk since leaving Halifax, Nova Scotia. The mood aboard ship was not a happy one as we contemplated the long, long journey across bleak seas. England – and home – was far away.

As I kept watch, I noticed that the commodore ship was signalling to something out on the horizon beyond us. I could but vaguely make out the silhouettes of what looked like warships. As they neared us and grew bigger I could eventually see that they were big ships. One in particular was very big, making a huge splash as she cut through the seas. My suspicions were soon confirmed by the commodore, who began signalling a general message to everyone. We were being instructed to keep strictly to our convoy-lane positions that kept us well away from the ships on either side of us. There had to be room for the naval flotilla to pass right down through our ranks. Usually the screening naval ships kept well away from the convoys, but this was to be something special, we could see. The large ship, to our astonishment, was not one of the usual destroyers employed to protect us, but the battleship HMS *Prince of Wales*. She and her escort had altered course to visit us; imagine, taking time to look at us.

We learnt that she was westward bound on important business, and aboard this prestigious ship was none other than Winston Churchill himself. Everyone came up on deck to see this naval pageant go by. The great ship majestically sailed down through the convoy lane that was immediately on our starboard side. As she went by she was flying a flag signal from her halyards, a message from Churchill to us. It read, 'England expects that every man will do his duty'. Yes, of course. That had been Nelson's message from his ship HMS *Victory* to his fleet, which had numbered only twenty-seven ships in all. Having sent this message to his loyal men, he had gone into battle against the combined fleets of France and Spain and won the day at Trafalgar on 21 October 1805. This, too, was Churchill's signal for victory to us.

What a feeling of elation it brought! Every man cheered and cheered and cheered. Churchill, the most famous First Lord of the Admiralty, was actually right there, in person, beside us. That day Nelson lived again among us! The spirit of victory was ours.

From that moment, all our fears of U-boats and torpedoes evaporated; for the rest of the trip home we were more courageous, if not braver, men.

Later in my sea adventures, when courage began to fail me, and that was not infrequently, I recalled that memorable occasion. That kind of inspiration reminded me that I had another leader, far greater than Churchill, right there beside me; he who has promised me the ultimate victory over every foe. So I would say to myself, 'What have I to fear, if he is with me?'

Chapter 9

Strange encounters

Some of the ancient ships that I sailed on could hardly be called luxury liners. One of those ships, a relic of the past, lacked even the most basic conveniences. To put it bluntly, on board was no running water for the use thereof, except for the heavy seas that filled her scuppers.

Drinking water was supplied each day, if the steward remembered, in a carafe-like water bottle, which was placed in a rack situated on top of what they called a toilet cabinet. On a hinged shelf of this cabinet there was a porcelain basin that had to be manually filled with water for washing. It then had to be emptied into a slop bucket and carried and emptied over the side of the ship. A knowledge of the leeward and windward sides of the ship was essential!

The toilet itself was a compartment located on the lower deck. There was running water of a kind, seawater from a saltwater tank.

One night I availed myself of this *in*convenience and in so doing suffered the shock of my life. When I flushed that toilet in the pitch darkness of the night (no lights were allowed because of the strict blackout), I was startled to see sparks of fire running through the flushing water – bright blue sparks, lighting up that dingy lavatory.

I learned that the sparks were really hundreds of minute crustaceans, or shellfish, that inhabited the salt water that had been pumped up from the sea outside into our salt-water tank. Later that night on deck I was to see millions of these creatures being boiled up by our propellers. They left a luminous wake behind our ship that reached all the way back to the horizon. I had never imagined that I would encounter sea fireflies in a ship's lavatory!

On another occasion, while we were lying at anchor off Cape Town, South Africa, I had another rather funny encounter. We spent some time there, off the entrance to the harbour, and whiled away the time doing a bit of fishing.

One afternoon, I borrowed a rod and began to descend the gangway down the side of the ship. The bottom plat-form of the gangway was just a few inches above the water. As I reached it, I sat down on the last step to prepare my rod and hooks.

Suddenly, there was a plop, a watery sounding plop, and sitting there right beside me at my feet was the cutest little penguin I had ever seen. Keeping very still, I looked at him and he at me. I expected him to plop off immedi-ately when he realised that he had come so perilously close to a human being. But no! He was just as interested in me as I was in him. There he stood, looking at me.

I ventured at last to say, 'Hello!' He said nothing. I don't know what penguins say anyhow. Instead, he eyed me up and down. Then, with some trepidation, I stretched for-ward and gently shook his little black flipper. Still he just looked at me in silence.

I kept speaking softly to him. I like to talk to God's creatures. I think we were meant to befriend them all.

Then, just as suddenly as he came, without as much as

a wink, he launched himself with a plop back into the sea again. He darted away under the water like a black arrow from a bow, and was gone.

I have often thought of that brief encounter with a real live penguin. I don't think he dashed off because he was afraid of me. He didn't see man as an enemy. In his part of the world penguins never meet humans and therefore were not afraid of them. Perhaps I was the first man he had seen and he wasn't impressed, or he was just bored with my conversation.

One doesn't expect a ship to be boarded in the middle of the ocean nowadays. Pirate days are long since gone. Yet I have encountered a few exceptions.

Once, off the Western Isles of Scotland, early one morning we noticed, high up in the cross trees of the mast, an unusual boarder. It was a lone owl. There he perched and remained with us right across the Atlantic. Many days later, early in the morning, we saw that he had gone, flown off in the night. Presumably he reached Canada before we did. I had a strange thought that crossed my mind. Can British owls speak the same owl language as Canadian owls? I wondered how he fitted into the environment of his new land.

There was another occasion when we were sailing down the Malabar coast on our way from Bombay to what used to be known as Ceylon. There we encountered another strange boarding of our ship. The greeny-blue Indian Ocean stretched out to the horizon around us.

I joined the navy to see the sea, as the song goes, and what did I see? I saw the sea! And more and more sea.

The monsoons were over, the heavy rain clouds gone and the sky above was a canopy of unblemished blue.

Then we saw it, a strange white cloud coming towards us. As it came it followed the surface of the sea. Then it was suddenly upon us, covering the ship from stem to stern. It was hundreds and hundreds of beautiful butterflies. Where they came from and where they were going nobody knew. Perhaps they were migrating somewhere, there on the mainland, and had been blown out to sea on some sudden tropical wind. Who knows? Alas! They all perished that night. Sadly, we swept their flimsy lifeless bodies into the sea, life and beauty gone in such a brief moment. But they had been beautiful to behold, even for such a short moment in time.

My next encounter occurred in the Mediterranean Sea. It happened when I was serving on a hospital ship. I have to explain that on such a ship we were supposedly immune from enemy attack and could operate our radios freely. Accordingly, we were busy doing our job as normal radio officers, communicating and transmitting radio messages throughout our watches.

One evening, just before sunset, one of our nursing sisters came bursting into the wireless room. She was extremely agitated. 'Please don't transmit any messages at the moment,' she implored me, 'you'll kill the birds!' With this outburst she grabbed my arm and pulled me out onto the deck, pointing me to something aloft. There they were, the birds, rows and rows of swallows perching the whole length of my wireless aerials. I could see her predicament. I laughed and tried to explain to her that the radio signals would not hurt them one little bit. There was no way that high frequency signals could pass through them to earth. They would have had to have one foot on the ground and one on the aerial for this to happen. The sister took a lot of convincing!

That flock of swallows was on its migratory journey from somewhere in Europe, perhaps even Britain, for its winter holidays in Africa. As evening was approaching, the birds had seen our twinkling lights below – hospital ships were like fairy castles at night – and had come down to rest on our rigging.

Out in Ethiopia I have witnessed swallows from home roosting for the night, and marvelled how such tiny birds could undertake such long journeys. Still more marvellously, how they could navigate their way home again, back to the very nesting place they had set out from. It seems to me that someone has implanted a wonderful guidance system into their tiny heads. Could it not be he who notes the sparrow fall? Who looks after me, too?

But for now, here is another strange encounter. This time it happened in New Zealand. I still laugh when I think about it.

Our voyage to the Antipodes took us over the Christmas period that year, and we had our festive dinner at sea. I mention this because one of the officer cadets featured in this story really disgraced himself at the Christmas dinner.

We fared very well at that party. The saloon table was groaning with an abundance of food. Soon, we in turn were also groaning from our over-indulgences! But there was a plum pudding left over and, knowing the young lad's insatiable appetite, we coaxed him into demolishing this last pudding in its entirety. Unfortunately, the 'Old Man' witnessed his bout of greedy bravado. The next morning, the morning after the night before, I met the cadet on deck. Instead of his usual spruce uniform he was wearing a boiler suit and was doing punishment detail. There he was in the boiling sun, sweating profusely. It is hot at Christmas time down under but, armed with a heavy hammer, he was chipping the metalwork on the deck and preparing it for red leading and painting. I was told that he had been ordered to work off the excess cargo he carried from his over-indulgence at the party.

Some of us seem to learn the hard way, and that unfortunate lad had yet another lesson to learn. He joined his mate and me on an expedition ashore when we reached New Zealand. It was my first time in that beautiful country, a new land and a new shore to explore. That day we walked along the beach, discovering new things and thoroughly enjoying good old 'terra firma'. Then, just where the waves gently ran up onto the sand, we saw them, lots and lots of the prettiest seashells. They were so attractive, so different from any I had seen before, that I decided to pocket a few to take home as souvenirs of New Zealand. The other lads were of the same mind and also began collecting. The aforementioned cadet, true to his nature, decided to run ahead of us along the beach so that he could pick the best shells before we reached them. Soon his pockets were bulging with his trophies, until suddenly he stopped, as if frozen on the spot. He was standing staring down at the same shells around his feet. Then, just as suddenly as he had frozen still, he began frantically to empty his pockets of all the shells he had gathered. I can see him now, pulling them out and vehemently throwing them to the sand. We caught up with him. He was shouting, 'Look! Look!' and pointing down to the shells around him. The pretty, innocent shells had come alive and were scurrying away in all directions on claws! We laughed and laughed and laughed. He had pocketed some shells that were the homes of very-much-alive hermit crabs!

It doesn't pay to pocket everything you see. I often wonder, after all those years, if that poor lad is still selfishly looking after 'number one' today.

Mind you, I, too, had a good look through the shells in my pockets that day to make sure that I hadn't made the same mistake!

Chapter 10

Hospital ship
St David

When I joined the hospital ship, the *St David*, I entered a new phase of my 'other world'. Till then I had mostly experienced the grey Atlantic days of slow convoys crawling across the ocean at the speeds of the slowest ships. Considering the age of the old tubs at sea in those days, that was a monotonously slow crawl; eight knots, perhaps. Then there were the menacing 'Wolf Packs' of U-boats and the fearful sinkings in freezing waters. Cruel seas they were indeed.

But the grey days were to undergo a sea change, and it would be different, I hoped. I didn't realise just *how* different it would be.

She was a beautiful ship, the *St David*. I joined her in Glasgow. Today, from the motorway into the city, I still see the cranes of the King George V docks where I first saw her.

There she was, a pristine white ship with a rakish yellow funnel. A band of green encircled her hull which was interspersed with red crosses. She looked so spectacularly different from the grey ships all around her. She was a queen! Until commissioned by the army, she had been a GWR cross-channel ferry with turbine-powered engines. She had a fair turn of speed. But the real joy to me was not in her looks or design; she was a free spirit, free, that is, from enemy intervention. As a hospital ship she was protected by the Geneva Convention and free from any kind of enemy attack. No more guns! No more torpedoes! A safe haven in a troubled sea. I couldn't believe my good fortune.

In the strength of this new-found freedom I went ashore from our anchorage in the Gareloch to Helensburgh, and there I bought myself a whole set of Charles Dickens books that I had been longing to buy. Previously it would have been too risky to take them to sea with me. They would only have joined the many other possessions of mine in Davy Jones's Locker.

Under orders as an army hospital carrier, in due course we found ourselves at the forefront of the Allied invasion of Sicily and Italy. It was during that campaign that still another world was to be opened to me. It was the horrible world of armed combat, man to man, gun to gun, and the bloody outcome of the bullet, and the shell, and the bombs, and that lethal shrapnel. Our carrier was to be the temporary refuge for the wounded lads who fell while scaling the beaches.

Even today, I still remember the smell of war, the sickly stench of gangrene that we couldn't rid ourselves of, in spite of the gallons of antiseptics we used. I remember, too, the dreadful but necessary amputations that our surgeons had to perform to save lives. There were also the canvas-shrouded bodies laid out on deck. I had to walk by those on my way to the wireless room.

That was the world of war in all its degradation; hardly the adventure I had hoped for so joyfully back in Glasgow. Yet there were times when we, as a hospital carrier, could pull away from the invasion fleets and enjoy a respite from the air raids out in the open sea. There we would tend to our wounded and, from time to time, set off to transport them to hospitals behind the lines.

Chapter 11

Lights along the shore

We were making an urgent voyage from the battle front in Italy to a base hospital in North Africa, and had on board a larger than normal number of casualties. Rather more than we cared to have. We were nearing our destination, our estimated time of arrival (ETA) about thirty minutes away, and I was on watch. We were singing along; the whine of the turbine engines indicating that they were on maximum revolutions. I had already looked out across the boat deck to see how we were progressing and, although night had set in, I could see that we were running along the coastline. Now and then a heavy rain squall would come down and obscure the view in front of us, but it would soon clear again. I could plainly see the beam from the lighthouse guiding us into port.

Suddenly I was alarmed by the ship's telegraph ringing down to the engine room. There was an instant answering ring from below and the whine of the turbine blades changed. I heard the stern turbine spring to life. Turbine engines cannot be reversed so a rear reverse turbine engine is there to propel the ship backwards. I could feel the propellers churning us astern. The ship shuddered violently. Running out on deck, I looked over the handrails and could see the boiling, frothing sea below us breaking over huge boulders right below our hull. We were pulling off a stone jetty that we had almost run into.

The story that unfolded was this. As I have mentioned, we had been following the guiding light of the lighthouse into the harbour. This time a rain squall had descended on us for a much longer time than usual, thus obscuring our line of approach. In that time we had drifted off course. Suddenly the officer on the bridge saw, through the heavy rain and mist, a line of lights; not the lighthouse, for it was still hidden, but little lights strung the length of the shore-line – and we were just about on top of them! He shouted the alarm and the helmsmen steered the ship away. So it was that we were saved by the lights along the shore.

During the gloomy black-out days of Britain at war there were no such promenade lights along the coast, only the big lights of the lighthouses that sent their welcoming beams out to us. We could see them miles out to sea, describing arcs on the horizon, showing us the way home. Over in Canada and the States we could still see the shore lights along the coasts. The big lights showed us the way, but it was the little lights that gave us the real welcome. The twinkling lights along the promenades and on the piers, the warm glowing lights in the windows of the houses by the sea. They meant homes, and people, and firesides, and friends, and everything that wasn't the dark and cold loneliness of the unfriendly sea.

I often think of the story I have just told you when we sing the hymn, 'Let the lower lights be burning'. It goes on: 'Brightly beams our Father's mercy from his lighthouse ever more; But to us he gives the keeping of the lights along the shore.' Yes, the little lights are important in the saving of souls. They saved *my* life.

I often tell children about the lighthouses I have met along the way and I like to share this little poem with them:

'I'd like to be a lighthouse
All scrubbed and painted white
I'd like to be a lighthouse
And stay awake all night
To keep my eye on everything
That sails my patch of sea;
I'd like to be a lighthouse
With the ships all watching me.'

Chapter 12

Chart
and compass

B ack in those halcyon days of peace, long before my sea stories began, when I was at high school I had a friend. Between this elderly lady and me there grew a strange relationship which was to influence greatly the choices I was to make during the dark days of wartime to follow.

At school in those days I was being initiated into the new thinking of the time, the scientific approach to all things. It wasn't quite the technology of today but the picture of school education was changing. Suffice it to say that the older generation around me were considered 'not quite with it', just as the youth around me today probably think that I, too, am a simple, poor old chap.

My friend, old Mrs Wingate, was to me a comical picture of a woman. I can see her now, dressed always in black as, of course, befitted a widow in those days. She wore a black shiny hat that hardly had any brim, from under which peeped a tight bun of grey hair, and the inevitable shawl hung over her bent shoulders. The old soul lived right by my school and I saw her nearly every day. She would be going around the neighbourhood from door to door carrying a large square straw basket, covered with a white linen cloth. She made her living selling home-made scones. I often popped in to see her, and the aroma of those griddle-baked scones filled her kitchen and made my mouth water. They were absolutely delicious. White soda ones, brown oatmeal ones and out-of-this-world, scrumptious treacle ones.

But as Mrs Wingate went from door to door she had more than appetising scones to offer her customers. She gave, free of charge, the Gospel message, and she offered it with such a beautifully disarming smile that nobody shut her door on Mrs Wingate.

She was a great friend of my mum's. My real mother had died when I was just an infant but Mum brought me up with a great deal of love.

For some reason, of which I had not a clue then, Mrs Wingate made it her business to come to our door rather more frequently than to her other customers. She would single me out in her conversation. She liked to hear my views on things, she would say, but her real purpose was to get me interested in reading the Bible. 'Have you seen this? or have you heard that?' she would ask, and 'What do you think about so and so?'

'Look, Mrs Wingate,' I would protest, 'I am about to sit for my Highers, and really don't have the time for this kind of study. Besides', I would add, 'these signs of the times you talk about are just old-fashioned ideas.'

I admit I would get ruffled by her persistence, although I really knew her intentions were kind concern for me and my future. I remember once when we truly entered into a real controversy about Bible Creationism and so-called Scientific Evolution. I was furiously defending science; after all, one of my Higher subjects was science and I had already been studying it for five years at high school, and, besides, what did she know about the formation of the earth? I thought.

It was then that I said some hard things to her in my anger and pride. I can still see the little tear that welled up and ran down her cheek, although she also tried to smile at me.

Even at that moment I felt ashamed of myself; but that pride of mine would not let me relent. I lost it with her, as they say today. And with a kindly word to me she quietly went away.

In her way, she was offering me a guide to the future, and trying to share with me the hope she had in that future she believed in.

Much later, during the cruel days that were to follow I was to think about what she had tried to show me. We all need a guide in life, but few of us like to be told. Nevertheless, there is a guideline outside of our own concepts that we would do well to look at sometimes.

Which reminds me of another short but poignant sea story of mine, this time about a captain, a commodore no less, who was greatly revered by those who sailed under him. I sailed with another commodore very much like him in the early days of my service. I had a problem, a very embarrassing problem for a so-called sailor. I was prone to seasickness. One day the commodore came into my wireless room, and to my shame he noticed that I was not quite myself. Probably it was my face that gave the show away. It was as white as a sheet. He looked at me and to my dismay, he smiled. 'Feeling queasy, Sparks?' he asked. 'Well, let me tell you something. I've been going to sea nearly all my life, and I still get seasick at the beginning of every trip.'

You know, I felt better immediately. Here was a big man who felt for the little men under his command.

Well, concerning the commodore of the story, it was

said that he had a peculiar habit that nobody understood. Apparently, aboard his ship, on the bulkhead at the back of the bridge, he had a little wooden box. It had a door that was always kept locked. Just now and again, but particularly when he was commanding ship manoeuvres, he would go to the box, open it, consult something inside it, close it and continue his orders. What was he referring to inside that box? It was too small to contain a map or a book. Just what was inside that mysterious box? In the end the commodore left the ship for duty elsewhere, but the box remained where it was. The key to open the box went with the great man. As you can imagine, curiosity killed the cat. The box was forced open to reveal its secret. Guess what the sailors found? Inside was a little white card about the size of a visiting card and on it was printed in bold letters the following:

PORT (RED) = LEFT　　STARBOARD (GREEN) = RIGHT

Like most of us, if we truly care to admit it, this brilliant man had trouble remembering things – in his case, the nautical names for left and right and the appropriate colours that indicated which was which! When under stress he would turn to that little wooden box for guidance. He didn't dare ask his officers to put him right on the matter. That would have been more than his pride was worth.

There is a secret place that we can all go to for guidance when we are stressed out. There is a chart and compass available to us all when our self-sufficiency is not adequate to meet the problems that come our way.

Mine I found to be my little blue Bible. I am also grateful for the simple admonition that was given to me by that wise old lady, Mrs Wingate, even though I had so callously rejected her.

Chapter 13

The parcel

The good ship *St David* took me on to a series of adventures. Some I shall never forget. Amid the serious, strange things of war there were also funny things that happened. We were, after all, human beings who could laugh as well as cry, and be amused as well as scared to death.

We were up in the port of Bari, in the Adriatic sea. It was a very busy port during the invasion of Italy. Because of the many ships there, we were obliged to moor to a buoy in the middle of the outer harbour. To go ashore we depended on a liberty boat to ship us to the quayside.

It was late in the evening; in fact it was the last boat from shore to ship, and aboard the liberty boat was a motley crowd of very drunk sailors. We ferried between moored ships, dropping off the lads at their prospective vessels until we came to the last but one ship. Ours was next.

As we drew alongside the companion way of this penultimate ship, I noticed a very inebriated Scotsman stagger to his feet with great difficulty for he was carrying a very bulky parcel under his arm. Keeping his balance and trying to keep hold of his parcel proved, in the end, to be too much for him.

There was a huge splash!

Both he and his parcel disappeared between the boat and the landing platform. In the meantime, his mates who were leaning over the rails of his ship watching the on-going circus with much mirth, burst into gleeful applause. Then I heard a voice shouting, 'Get his parcel!' When the parcel was fished out of the briny and was up on deck a long time before the bedraggled sailor, I had to ask myself, what was more important? The man or the parcel?

I recalled how, when my first ship went down, the shipping authorities had terminated my wages. Remuneration was evidently available only to those in active service. For the week I spent in a lifeboat trying to survive without food in the middle of the ocean, I was considered to be unemployed and not worthy of wages. The powers-that-be had lost their ship and I suppose I had to sympathise with them. But what about the poor seamen? Sometimes it is a hard, materialistic world, this world of ours.

Funny things did happen, as on that crazy night ashore in Bari, but tragedies were more frequent. That same night the Germans laid mines in the harbour entrance.

Early next morning, at breakfast time, we were alarmed by a terrific explosion beyond the harbour. Rushing out onto deck, we were just in time to see one of our mine-sweepers sinking in the channel. We helped rescue the crew, pulling wounded lads into our sea ambulances. The minesweeper herself had run foul of some new kind of mine she had not been able to handle.

We were called to leave Bari that day. Gingerly, because of all the mines, we made our way down the channel, all of us wearing lifebelts until we were safely out to sea.

But that night, 2 December 1943, one of the most costly engagements of the war in the Mediterranean, and one seldom mentioned in World War Two histories, occurred at that Italian port of Bari on the Adriatic.

At that time, the British 8th Army was pushing the enemy back along the coast. The thirty freighters that we had just harboured with were discharging ammunition, bombs, gasoline and other supplies needed for the drive north.

At about 20:30 aircraft engines were heard. Winches stopped as searchlights probed the moonlit sky. Guns on all the ships were manned and ready, and parachute flares lit up the harbour. Enemy aircraft were overhead.

Suddenly, all hell rained down on those ships bottled up in the harbour.

The battle might have lasted only twenty minutes, but at the end of it seventeen ships had been sunk or damaged beyond repair. The harbour was filled with wreckage. Flaming oil burned many men to death as they tried to swim away from their sinking ships. Ammunition ships blew up and rolled over in the water; decks ripped open. The British ship *Athabaska*, carrying two captured 1,000-pound German rocket bombs, caught fire, blew up and sank. Forty-four men from her fifty-six-man crew perished.

The battle of Bari is long past, and some have never even heard about it.

Some of us will never forget it.

Chapter 14

Who is the enemy?

A s far as we aboard the hospital ship *St David* were concerned, the invasion of Sicily had gone tolerably well. The landing didn't result in a great deal of work for us, casualty-wise. We lay anchored offshore awaiting the call for our sea ambulances, which were always at the ready. We shipped them as we would normally in the lifeboat davits on the boat deck.

But things changed, as they so often do in warfare. Suddenly we and the other support ships anchored beside us were under attack from two hilltops above the southern Sicilian harbour where we were landing. The enemy fire was from the dreaded 88 mm guns; fast and accurate,  and they were blasting us with shrapnel shells. We moved around the anchorage to divert the attacks; our funnel riddled with holes. Pieces of red-hot shrapnel even came belting down into my wireless room.

Our naval destroyers did their best, but still every now and again we all had to keep our heads down and stop commuting between harbour and shore. Darkness stopped the on-slaught of those well-dug-in enemy gun emplacements and we had a little respite under the cover of night.

Very early the next morning, just before daybreak, I saw a wonderful sight. Coming in from the sea behind us was one of our greatly beloved capital ships. She sailed down past our stern, turned about, and began to steam, still keeping behind us. I saw her gun turrets turn shoreward and saw the flashes and yellow smoke billowing forth from the mouths of their mighty cannon, and heard the roar of those very accurate shells as they soared over our mastheads.

I turned to look shoreward; up towards the enemy gun emplacements on the hills. At each location there arose a large plume of smoke, followed by an almighty volcanic eruption with columns of smoke and fire rising high up into the morning sky. The gun emplacements were reduced to holes in the hillside. I turned round once more to watch that mighty ship quietly but majestically making her way back out to sea, en route to some other engagement. All around were cheers that split the morning air as we rejoiced in our deliverance.

That day we went ashore safely, no shells exploding around us. We were met with welcoming arms by the Sicilian townsfolk; they, too, were happy to be free from their late army occupation. We made our way up to the town square. Hordes of grateful people were surrounding the Cathedral to say thanks to God for their freedom, or so I presumed. A group, mostly of women, drew our attention, particularly as we could hear a frenzied wail coming from their midst. Pushing our way through the crowd, we were confronted by a terrible sight. A poor young woman was tearing at her clothes and hair while, only a short distance away, a young girl was witnessing her mother totally mad and in shock from the shelling.

Our victorious shells had done more than destroy two enemy gun emplacements. I felt so ashamed I could have torn the epaulettes from my shoulders.

There is no real victory in the death, destruction and devastation in wartime. War itself is the evil enemy on both sides of any conflict.

Chapter 15

Somebody else's blood

We hear remarkable stories of men of bravery and daring, and selfless deeds of sacrifice on the battlefield, and we wonder if the stories can really be true. How can thinking men do such things? Yet from the wee bit of bravery that I was privileged to see, it was expected of soldiers and sailors every day. The men who performed such acts of bravery were just lads doing a job of duty, and sometimes they were not so much afraid of the job as they were of not doing it right and disappointing the officer in command. There are few things more frightening than an officer's bark!

From early on in the beach landings there remains with me a picture that I will never forget.

We were running our sea ambulances onto a particular shoreline along with a large army landing craft. The lads were wading from the ramps of their craft up onto the beach when I heard the sound of a piper and there, in the midst of the boys, was a much younger looking lad with his bagpipes bursting under his arm and his kilt floating in the moving tide. No gun, just a skirl of Scottish music that said, 'Come on, lads, up and at 'em.' I will never know what happened to that wee lad in those terrible days, but that day he was a hero for sure.

As the real fighting intensified, so casualties increased. The hospital ship spent as long as she could near the shore until our complement of wounded became too great. We deck officers did our usual watches and, when not on watch, we helped out below decks with the wounded and injured. I assisted in the reception ward, just behind the sally-port or entrance to the main deck of the ship where the sea ambulances brought in the stretcher cases. It was our job at reception to ascertain what wounds they had received and then to send them on to the appropriate place for medical attention. A stretcher-bound lad was brought to my table. As I removed the red blanket that covered him, I saw a young lad, his face white and gaunt and his eyes full of fear. He was in shock, but I couldn't help noticing that he still had his 9lb rifle firmly in his grasp. No one had been able to part him from his gun.

'Come on, son,' I said. 'Let me have your gun. You won't be needing it for a wee while.'

He firmly resisted my freeing him from it. I could just imagine what was going through his head – a sergeant shouting at him, 'Don't you ever let go of that gun. That's the most important thing in your life, treat it with reverence, or else!' We did finally manage to get rid of the ruler of his life.

Not very long after that, our roles were reversed and I was the one being brought through the sally-port of our sister hospital ship after the *St David* was sunk.

I, too, was laid out on the table to have my injuries assessed. When they pulled the blanket from me the right leg of my uniform was soaked in blood. They cut away my trousers and somebody said, astonished, 'There isn't a scratch to be seen anywhere! You're lucky, Sparks. It must have been somebody else's blood. You must have picked it up from somebody you were helping in the sea.' And so it was.

Perhaps this was one of the greatest lessons of life that I have ever learned. To my mind, I have not been a great achiever in my lifetime, but one thing that I have succeeded in and succeeded well in, is being a *survivor*! But no Brownie points to me for that. Somebody has looked after me – he who gave his blood for me.

Yes, Somebody else's blood is there for *everybody's* salvation, whoever we may be.

Chapter 16

Missiled
off Anzio

To speed up the slow pace of the Allied northward advance through Italy, against the fierce German defences at Casino and the Gustav Line, strategists planned a landing behind the German lines. On 22 January 1944 the British and American troops launched a successful surprise attack and landing on the Anzio beachhead. But soon, within the congested invasion perimeter, casualties began to mount as the Allies were persistently pounded by ground attacks and a new kind of menace from the air.

The Germans had always shown the greatest interest in developing new sorts of weapons, and in the field of guided missiles were far ahead of the Allies. One of the earliest guided missiles to go into service was the Henschel HS293, which was launched from a parent aircraft and then guided to its target by radio. The missile's Walther rocket motor developed a maximum thrust of 1,250lbs, which gave the weapon a speed of 375 mph with a warhead weighing 725lbs.

The night after General Schlemmer's appointment to the German Anzio command, the Luftwaffe made a damaging attack on the shipping in the harbour. Already the quays and the anchorages had been submitted to intermittent shelling. Then dive-bombers came into the attack on the crowded shipping with aerial torpedoes and the newly-invented radio-controlled guided bombs, along with armour-piercing bombs weighing 2,500lbs.

By 24 January 1944 the 33rd field hospital and the 95th and 96th evacuation hospital had been set up and quickly went into operation. Approximately 200 nurses had been assigned to these units. Our nurses from the *St David* were known as the Queen Alexandra Imperial Medical Nursing Staff; super girls in their grey uniforms with red borders and their white capes, who worked so hard as they received the wounded from the shore. It was a hectic time for us all.

We were three hospital ships under the command of the 8th Army – HMS *St Andrew*, HMS *Leinster* and my ship HMS *St David*. It was late in the evening of 24 January.

I had just come up on deck after dinner and was walking along the boat deck, going towards the wireless room.

The chief was on duty. His watch was 8 to 12.

Suddenly I wasn't on deck any more but up in the air and then back down again and on my back.

It came back to me all too quickly; it had happened once more. We had been hit.

The strange phenomenon of hearing no sound meant that whatever explosion had taken place was too near to be heard; but my head was singing.

The stunned silence over, I came to and rose to my feet to face the situation around me. I could see that we were sinking rapidly. Crewmen were frantically trying to lower the lifeboats manually as there was no electric power for the winches. Torchlights were flashing and men shouting to one another.

My job was to get the portable emergency transmitter

into a lifeboat so I ran to fetch it from the wireless room. I could see our chief busy with the SOS procedure. Back at the first lifeboat I was alarmed to see that it was still in the davits but already sinking into the sea.

George, our officers' steward, went by me to go below. 'Don't!' I shouted. 'You must swim for it!'

'Oh, but I have a duty down there,' he mumbled in a daze, and disappeared below.

At the other end of the boat deck I could see the captain at the top of the companion way on the bridge, his Mae West on, and his tin helmet with 'Captain' written on it in white letters.

Oh, yes, I had been in that situation before. Only one thing for it. Over the side and swim like mad – and don't get caught in the down pull when she goes under.

It was January and the sea was cold, very cold indeed. There were other souls who needed help, swimming with me, struggling in the water, and the coldness of the water was not important just then.

After an eternity help came. Over the dark waves lifting us up and down, obscuring things immediately on the surface, appeared the multi-coloured fairy lights of one of our companion hospital ships. Though damaged herself, the HMS *Leinster* had managed to make her way towards us.

In a few brief minutes our *St David* was gone with many of the 226 medical staff and patients plus the ship's crew. Only 130 of us survived.

Gone was our quiet and respected captain, who had carried out naval tradition: standing on the bridge, he had gone down with his ship. Gone was George, forever thinking of his duty to others, who had often nipped up from the galley in the long dark hours of the midnight watch with a poached egg on toast just for me (though I knew he was a special friend to *all* the officers). I often recall that diminutive, uniformed gentleman, and gentleman he was, disappearing back down the inside companion way, to do his duty and meet his death. I can't forget that young, wounded soldier whom I had parted from his rifle. Sadly, I had been right. He had never needed it again.

Like so many shipmates and friends, they come to mind time and time again when the sad memories from the past surge up from the subconscious mind. As the poet Laurence Binyon says in his *Valediction*:

> 'With proud thanksgiving, a mother for her children,
> England mourns for her dead across the sea.
> Flesh of her flesh they were, spirit of her spirit,
> Fallen in the cause of the free.
> They shall not grow old, as we that are left grow old:
> Age shall not weary them, nor the years condemn.
> At the going down of the sun and in the morning,
> We will remember them.'
> *(Verses 1 and 4, from The Golden Treasury)*

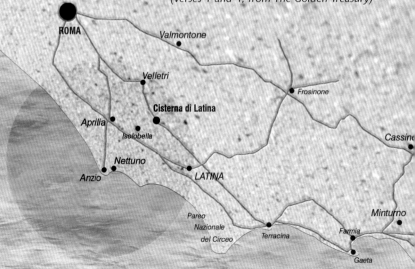

Chapter 17

Sandcastles

My 'Mum', bless her, not my real mother sadly, as mentioned earlier, but the best and only mother I ever knew, used to have a strange and recurring dream. A dream that caused her great anxiety concerning me. She would tell me about it as I sat on her knee as a little boy. Even when I was a 'grown up' lad she reminded me of it.

In her dream she would be with me by the seaside. She would be watching me building sandcastles, as we often did together. 'Let's build them as near to the sea as we can,' we used to say. Then we would wait and watch for the incoming tide to rush and fill the moats we had dug around them. Of course, the sea always won, and the fragile sandcastles toppled into the oncoming sparkling, bubbling wavelets, and very soon they were no more. All our hectic building and sculpturing for nothing! The downfall of the castles did not matter in those carefree days. There was always another sunny day beside the sea to build another sandcastle, perhaps a bigger, stronger one the next time.

But one day, in her dream, Mum saw her little boy in grave danger. She saw him building his castle, but she saw what he did *not* see. The sea that was filling his moat and giving him so much fun was also surrounding the beach where he was and cutting him off from the shore. In the dream that was to become a nightmare for her, she rushed out to save him, throwing herself into the sea, which was deep and which also separated them. But her dream ended there. Would she save him? Or would the sea take him away from her forever?

'Be careful of that sea, Son,' she would say. 'Don't trust it ever!'

Maybe it was her words of warning or maybe not, but I have always had a respectful fear of the sea. Even on the day that I learned to swim in Kirkcaldy harbour, when I learned to conquer its depths and keep my head above its surface, I learned that that was not mastery over it. Since then I have seen strong swimmers swim, but swim in vain, and watched as the heartless sea claimed their lives. Brave shipmates, dear friends. In my five years at sea I loved it but feared it. It was always a love-hate relationship.

We are assured that one day the sea will give up the dead it has claimed. During the awful conflict of the Second World War, the sea took for itself one in every four merchant seamen who dared to cross its waves, and many a mother's dream became a nightmare.

One day, that same 24 January 1944, my Mum was sitting alone at tea, listening to the six o'clock news, when suddenly she heard that the hospital ship *St David* had been sunk off Anzio. It was hot propaganda news to broadcast how deliberately and callously the enemy had broken the Geneva Convention and sunk defenceless hospital ships. The obligatory notification of next of kin before the release of fatal news was totally disregarded for propaganda purposes.

Mum realised the awful truth. Her own son was aboard that ship. Her fearful dream had come to pass. In agony of heart she waited to hear of my fate. It was left to me personally to let her know that I was all right. I sent her a telegram from Naples after I was discharged from hospital, saying, 'I'm coming home.' Poor soul, she never did get over this wounding shock and, not very long afterwards, it told on her life.

Chapter 18

Homecoming

As I said earlier, I don't feel I have been a great achiever in life, but I have been a great survivor.

As a survivor from the *St David*, I spent a little time in hospital in Naples, not the sunny Naples we sing about, but a wintry January Naples with snow on Mount Vesuvius.

We shipped home at last on the Dutch troopship *Tegelberg*. It was strange sailing as a passenger, but very enjoyable. Going home after a year, that was real joy.

Once before, I had had to be kitted out after losing everything when sunk on the MV *Rothley*, but that was in the tropics. This time it was the Army in Naples that found clothes to send me home in. 'Comic Cuts' would have had a field day if they had been allowed to take pictures of my going-home kit.

Let's see how smart I was. The underwear I will not describe. There was a khaki officer's shirt that was supposed to have a collar attached to it, but since there were no collars, I tied up a couple of khaki handkerchiefs to give the illusion. There was a fairly tight-fitting battledress, ample army socks, and much more ample and stiffer army boots. How on earth the poor soldiers got them to bend, I shall never know. Perhaps that is why they stamp their feet so much. But then the *piece de resistance*, an enormous army greatcoat that I virtually disappeared into. The lapels covered my ears and the bottom touched my boots. The winter chills of England would never get anywhere near me; so off we sailed from Naples and I was going home.

Our arrival in the Firth of Clyde and our sail up the river to Glasgow was an experience in itself. Seeing the well-kint [well-known] landmarks we had left behind what seemed like an eternity ago, did things to all of our hearts and eyes, especially to those soldiers who had served long in the North Africa Campaign and then in Italy.

We sailed by the old Cloche lighthouse, the guardian angel of the Clyde, then through the submarine boom, after signal lights had given us the OK to pass through. We were truly sailing up the Clyde, back to bonnie Scotland where all the 'old folks bide'. Passing Gouroch, Greenock and the port of Glasgow, lying behind myriads of ships of every description, but all grey, we moved on up the river and, as the waters narrowed, we could see the faces of the folks on the shore. By that time there were no boys left below deck. Everybody was hanging on the rails.

We moved past busy industries that had workers out waving to us as we sailed slowly by, and of course a great number were Scottish lassies in their overalls. As they shouted and blew kisses, there was a natural rush of the lads on deck to see them more closely. Consequently, as big as she was, the ship would list heavily in the same direction. From the bridge there suddenly sounded an alarm; loud hailers proclaimed orders for the troops to move well back from the rails and to give the crew a chance to dock the ship in a vertical position. What a day it was!

My job was done. Free from the regimentation of army

orderlies and the like, I went ashore. Before I reached the gangway, however, hastily scribbled letters were pushed into my hands. 'Post this for me, mate, as soon as you can.' It cost me a few stamps, but it was worth it. I dutifully reported to the Marconi office and was given a chit to present to the ticket office at Queen Street Station and there I would be given a ticket home.

I was quite surprised to see that my ticket was a white ticket and not the usual green one. This was a first class ticket! So I and my greatcoat and boots, and my exclusive first class ticket, wandered onto the platform. It was like wonderland.

The train was waiting. The crowds milled. The platform was heaped high with kitbags, cases, trunks and parcels, all to be manhandled by porters who looked as if they might ask, any moment, 'Is your journey really necessary?' Travellers, troops and civilians alike all looked for that precious seat or a decent place in the corridor. I didn't rush; a white ticket gets you anywhere. I looked for a carriage door that was not being assailed by the crowds and found myself an exceptionally empty compartment – top of the range travel. For a moment I almost forgot that I was going home. It was so nice to go, to go anywhere like this, sitting on those blue, plush-cushioned seats.

My bliss was suddenly interrupted.

The carriage door opened and in climbed an immaculately uniformed army officer. As he turned around to close the door behind him, I could see his shiny brown belt. Sitting down opposite me he placed a briefcase on the seat next to him and, taking a new hardback novel from under his arm, he proceeded to find his page. I imagined he was somebody from headquarters. From his uniform and shiny buttons it looked as if he had never seen conflict. He didn't speak, and nor did I, but a strange, uncomfortable atmosphere began to develop in the compartment. The whistle went and so did the train, gathering speed through the tunnel out of Queen Street Station and on to Kirkcaldy. The strange atmosphere intensified and I began to feel still more uncomfortable. Then almost undetected I saw his eyes take a quick peek over the top of his book. Yes, there he did it again. I pretended to look out of the window. Watching him furtively, I became aware that I was watching myself mirrored in the glass of the window and it suddenly dawned on me. My big army greatcoat; that was what he was looking at!

Feeling as though I was breaking through the enemy line, I said, 'Excuse me, sir, I think I had better explain something to you.' He dropped his book on his lap and looked rather pink and abashed. 'What you see isn't quite what it is.' I explained how I had come by my unbecoming outfit. Absolute relief changed his features as I told the story and we laughed together. 'You know,' he said, 'I was just wondering how I was going to put you on charge and what next I would have to do with you. A man isn't always what his clothes make him appear to be.' I was a sailor not a soldier and so the glasshouse lost out on another new recruit!

The train sped on, clickety-click. Those were the days before welded rail joints. Then the sound changed. We were crossing the Forth Bridge, that world-famous cantilever bridge that spanned the River Forth. I looked down on the grey choppy sea, as I had done on many a day when I had crossed over from the Kingdom of Fife on my way to college in Edinburgh. Once I remembered crossing over as the great battleship HMS *Hood* passed below. The pride of our navy, she was now sunk with all hands except for three poor seamen. That was a tragedy that we sailors would never forget.

Leaving the bridge, we passed by the naval graveyard of Inverkeithing. There, before the war, I had seen the scrapyard funeral of some of the great ships of World War I: the *Iron Duke*, flagship of Admiral Beatty, the famous *Lion* and *Tiger*.

Arriving in Kirkcaldy was a very peculiar experience. This mile-long town, with every kind of industry that you can mention, had one that it was very famous for, the linoleum industry. There were several factories throughout the town, and one in particular, Barry Olsten and Shepherds, whose tall factory buildings completely surrounded the railway station. It was not only the buildings that encompassed the station, but that awful smell of boiled linseed oil and paint that went into the unique floor covering called linoleum.

There's a memorable poem written about a wee boy coming to visit his grandma that ends with the line, already quoted: 'I know right well by the queer-like smell, the next stop is Kirkcaldy.'

Then I am home at last. The carriage door bangs behind me as I step onto that old familiar platform. Nothing has changed, only the faces of the people around me. That is something that disturbs me; the kint faces seem to disappear from the old familiar places each time I come back. Now it's only a fifteen-minute walk home.

It was with a rather quickened step that I made the last leg of the journey. I saw nothing as I walked on – the streets, the people – what I was looking for was in my mind. Then suddenly I was there. Before me were the outside stone steps leading up to the door, then the door and the brass bell-pull. I could hear the tinny sound of the bell tinkle in the hall. I had no key with which to let myself in. A seemingly endless wait, then the door opened and there was dear old Mum. There was a moment of silence as we confronted each other, then unstoppable tears and a wonderful hug that I wished would last forever.

At that moment in time, I had nothing except a give-away comic uniform, and yet I had everything.

It was one of those rare moments of life, a moment of utter contentment, something that winning the lottery would never give.

How did it feel?

I felt that my journey was over. I didn't want to be anywhere else.

I didn't want a new uniform or suit. There was just nothing else of material value that I wanted on earth, and I was once again just me, standing on my own doorstep. Unlike the prodigal son, I hadn't taken my father's riches away with me when I went off to that other world, but, like the prodigal son, I brought little more than rags back home.

One thing I do know. The great Father who truly loves me brought me home. What greater reward could I have wanted?

Chapter 19

Beyond the horizon and another world

My story started when I was a teenager. The things I had been learning at school had made me feel a bit more learned than some of the folks around me – the pals who had not gone through high school, the older generation who had seemed 'not quite with it'. Having no brothers or sisters, I had been surrounded by older people. There had been my Mum, who had brought me up and who had been good, kind and loving, but who had never played games with me. There had been the old lady, though not nearly as old as I am now, Mrs Wingate, a widow, who played with me in a funny kind of way. She had always been there in our home and, in the kindest way possible, she had tried to tell me of a better world to come. I hadn't wanted a better world to come. I hadn't wanted to read the magazines she had tried to push into my hand, especially the ones with pictures of angels in them. I had thought I knew better about the creation of the world; after all, I had a Higher in science! Yet there had been something about that poor old soul that had plagued me. I use that word because, like a plague, it had never left me. Her simple happiness and assurance in God had pervaded her whole being. I'll tell you a wonderful story about her in a page or two.

The Second World War had taken ships into uncharted waters, far away from the usual trade routes. We had had to find passages out of the range of enemy submarines; even for the regular crews a voyage had been a voyage of discovery. For me it had been an absolute adventure. What lay beyond?

Back on the shoreline of home, on many a clear summer's day, I had watched a ship coming up over the horizon. First I could see only the masts, then the funnels, then the hull of the ship. It's a round earth we live on; that's for sure. Approaching islands out to sea, you first observe a great mountain, its precipitous sides sticking up out of the ocean. Soon the land begins to surround the mountain and you realise that there is a shore where you can tie alongside.

I admire the bravery of our pioneer sailor adventurers who were willing to take the chance of falling off the edge of a supposedly flat world. Explorers often set out to find one place only to discover so many other places on the way. Captain James Cook is a particular hero of mine. He never did find Antarctica, but there are legends and tales and even maps drawn by some who did get there, long, long ago.

We have our charts and compasses, but the great thrill is to leave the chartroom and come out onto the bridge and virtually scan the horizon to see the land itself. We look for signs. Eyes, ears and noses all come into play. Noses, did I say? Yes, you can smell the land, that seaweedy smell that sailors recognise as 'the smell of land'. Out above the horizon you can see the sign of the clouds that form above land and then, as you get closer, you hear the mighty ocean surfing on the rocks. But even sailors can be fooled by the things around them.

Many years ago, in the days of sailing ships, a galleon had buffeted her way across the south Atlantic, journeying to South America, but making such slow progress that she ran out of supplies, especially fresh water. Things were desperate. Then one morning they sighted another ship coming towards them. The signalman was brought to the bridge and a request was made for fresh water. A reply came back, 'Dip down where you are.' Frantically the captain signalled again. 'It is fresh water we require; we are desperate.' Back came the same reply, 'Dip down where you are.' A simple little deck boy threw overboard a bucket tied to a rope, and pulled up some sea water. But when he tasted it, it was fresh water. The stricken ship was, in fact, away up the Amazon estuary and, although they could not see the land, they were surrounded by *fresh* water.

I, too, am learning to look down at the basics of life itself and to accept the signals and believe others who know better than me. That simple old soul whom I had disbelieved knew a lot more than I did. She had tried to tell me about another world that lay beyond today's horizon. She had called it the New Earth.

In the book she loved best, the Bible, there is a book within the many books which is called Revelation. It's the one at the very end. It tells of such a world to come, a world beyond the horizon of our present time.

Our world today is full of beautiful things, and enquiring men and women keep finding more and more wonders, but, in spite of all the efforts so admirably made to preserve and protect the good, there is another force at work to destroy. Our old world today is changing, and not for the better. There is turmoil and radical change in the world of nature – storms, earthquakes and climatic changes not seen before. But in the world of men the changes are even more evident. Jesus Christ, God's Son and the greatest prophet of all time, prophesied that there would be wars, and rumours of wars; nations would strive against nations; there would be famines and plagues, but he said that all those events would only be signs of a far greater event, the most wonderful event of all time, his second coming and the creation of a New World.

In the book of Revelation that I referred to, the writer, John, sees the end of our present world as it is, and by inspiration relates in chapter 21 verse 1, 'Then I (John) saw a new heaven and a new earth; for the first heaven and the first earth had passed away, and the sea was no more.'

No more storms and howling winds, no more fearful hurricanes, bombs and torpedoes, screaming, drowning men and death. Many times I had huddled in fear, silently wishing that it would soon be over. It will be over for us all one day soon, and there will be a new world so different from this one.

Going home, 'Sailing up the Clyde, back to bonnie Scotland, where the old folks bide', for me changed the whole picture. There was that sense of relief and inner joy. I used to feel it when I walked down the gangplank of the petrol tankers I sailed on, filled with their deadly cargoes – a burden of fear that I hadn't really wanted to recognise had fallen from my shoulders.

'Going home', how beautiful those two words are!

Mrs Wingate, poor soul, eked out her scanty subsistence with the sale of home-made scones around her neighbourhood. I can see her now with her basket over her arm, a little old lady passing by. She fell very ill, and some friends went to visit her. She shared her home with another widowed friend. It was she who opened the door to the two visitors and sadly told them that Mrs Wingate was at the end of her time, in a deep sleep and passing into that land of no communication. Nevertheless, they were invited in to see her. The friend bustled off to the room beyond and left them to visit quietly on their own. Suddenly one of the visitors came running to her, calling urgently, 'Come quickly! Mrs Wingate is trying to speak.' Her dear friend came instantly and, after leaning over the dying soul, said to the visitors, 'No, she's not speaking. She's singing her favourite hymn.' Thus Mrs Wingate left her friends, going to her rest to await the greatest joy of all; the call to another world beyond.

Down through the years I have had the privilege of sharing with others their hopes and troubles, their fears, and also their joys. Many have left before me, I am still going down the gangway. No, not going *down*, going *up*. I say to you as I have said to them, 'See you in the morning', in 'God's soon-coming Morning', in that 'Other World' beyond the horizon of our time.

Editor's Note

R. M. A. (Bob) Smart joined the navy to fight the foe and to see the world.

Home from the sea, he concluded that the real foe had been the war itself. And that it was in the values of his Kirkcaldy home that the seeds of another world, whose King was Jesus Christ, were to be found.

Having committed to the cause of Christ, Bob Smart left Kirkcaldy again. This time he went to Newbold College to train for ministry. There he met and married Joy.

Bob's ministry began on Humberside, but took in Ethiopia as well as a variety of cities in England and Ireland, and his native Scotland.

Many, including some well-known pastors, committed to Christ as a result of the Smarts' productive ministry.

This book is, in no small way, the result of the encouragement of Iris Smart and the hard work of Malcolm Smart, Bob and Joy's daughter and son.

Log book excerpts

Born in Kirkcaldy in the kingdom of Fife of the Clan McKenzie.

Mother died in my infancy. Fostered by Mum and Papa Cowper. Papa away engineering in foreign parts, Africa, Asia, Saigon, Sokoto, Singapore, so there was usually only Mum and me.

Education – primary and high school. Roll call at the infant school, the 'Red' School in Kirkcaldy was to me an embarrassment : surname followed by my Christian name – Smart Robert. It made me cringe. I had an uncle called Alex. I often wondered how he felt at roll call!

The Second World War loomed and I made a decision to escape parade ground bashing. Enrolled in the Edinburgh Wireless College. Gained a Post Masters Certificate in Wireless Telegraphy. Found a post with Marconi International Marine Communications Company Limited. Went to sea with Anglo Saxon Petroleum Company as a radio officer on a tanker at the tender age of 17.

It was then, and for the next five years, that I entered that 'other world'. My stories will have partly filled you in on that experience.

An old crew mate of mine who, like me, had his boots filled too many times with salt water, made a promise to himself. 'After the war,' he said, 'I shall grab an oar from a lifeboat and walk away from the sea – until I get so far inshore that no one I meet recognises what this oar is used for!'

So I too walked away and entered yet *another* world: Newbold Missionary College, where I trained for the ministry. I don't blame them, but I don't think Newbold was quite ready for 'Barnacle Bob' just home from the sea!

Of course, I was accepted, finally, and found so much

there. One thing I found was Joy, Joy Howard, my lovely soul mate. From then on my sailing suddenly caught a new, brisk, following breeze!

I signed off from Newbold in 1949, my discharge certificate tied with a black and yellow ribbon, having made many good lifelong friends and having learnt to know so much more of my dearest Friend of all.

My work was a battle for souls instead of a battle for survival in the grey North Atlantic, a battle no less real, but with a Captain like my Master, there was always going to be final victory.

As at sea, I changed shipmates and crews along the way. Some of my mentors passed their Christian seamanship on to me. They were numerous and a blessing to me, but just let me mention a few. There was Pastor John McMillan, who baptised me in Glasgow, Pastor Ken Elias, who taught me evangelism, and Pastor O. M. Dorland, who was the pastor's pastor for me and my family in Ireland.

I ministered and campaigned in Ireland, Scotland and many parts of England. I only managed camping in Wales, but I did get as far as Eritrea and Ethiopia, where we stayed for five years.

Iris, our daughter, came to us in Belfast, and Malcolm, or son, in Glasgow. They made up the full complement of our crew. A family that roughed the storms with Mum and Dad, for which I thank the Lord always.

Now I have joined the ranks of the senior citizens and find fellowship with some of my old pals in the lovely Scottish town of Crieff. I am not dropping anchor just yet for I believe with all my heart that the very best is yet to come, when Jesus appears over that horizon.

Signing off
Bob Smart

Bob's
sketch boards